NEW YORK

NEW HAMPSHIRE

MAINE

MASSACHUSETTS

Boston

CONNECTICUT

Providence

RHODE
ISLAND

N. York

Philadelphia

NEW JERSEY

ANIA

N O R T H

A T L A N T I C

O C E A N

FIRST FREEDOM

The Fight for Religious Liberty

For my brothers—Ken, David, Brian, and Mark
R. B.

In memory of Al Mabry—God Bless America
M. M.

❧

ALSO BY RANDALL BALMER:

The Making of Evangelicalism: From Revivalism to Politics and Beyond
God in the White House: How Faith Shaped the Presidency from John F. Kennedy to George W. Bush
Thy Kingdom Come: How the Religious Right Distorts the Faith and Threatens America
Religion in American Life: A Short History [CO-WRITTEN WITH JON BUTLER AND GRANT WACKER]
Protestantism in America [CO-WRITTEN WITH LAUREN F. WINNER]
Encyclopedia of Evangelicalism
Growing Pains: Learning to Love My Father's Faith
Religion in Twentieth Century America
Blessed Assurance: A History of Evangelicalism in America
Grant Us Courage: Travels Along the Mainline of American Protestantism
The Presbyterians [CO-WRITTEN WITH JOHN R. FITZMIER]
Mine Eyes Have Seen the Glory: A Journey into the Evangelical Subculture in America
A Perfect Babel of Confusion: Dutch Religion and English Culture in the Middle Colonies

Jacket and book design by Jessica A. Warner © 2012 Covenant Communications, Inc.

Published by Covenant Communications, Inc., American Fork, Utah

Printed in China
First Printing: October 2012

19 18 17 16 15 14 13 12   10 9 8 7 6 5 4 3 2 1

ISBN 978-1-60861-907-8

FIRST FREEDOM

The Fight for Religious Liberty

Companion book to the PBS Documentary

RANDALL BALMER ~ LEE GROBERG ~ MARK MABRY

TABLE OF CONTENTS

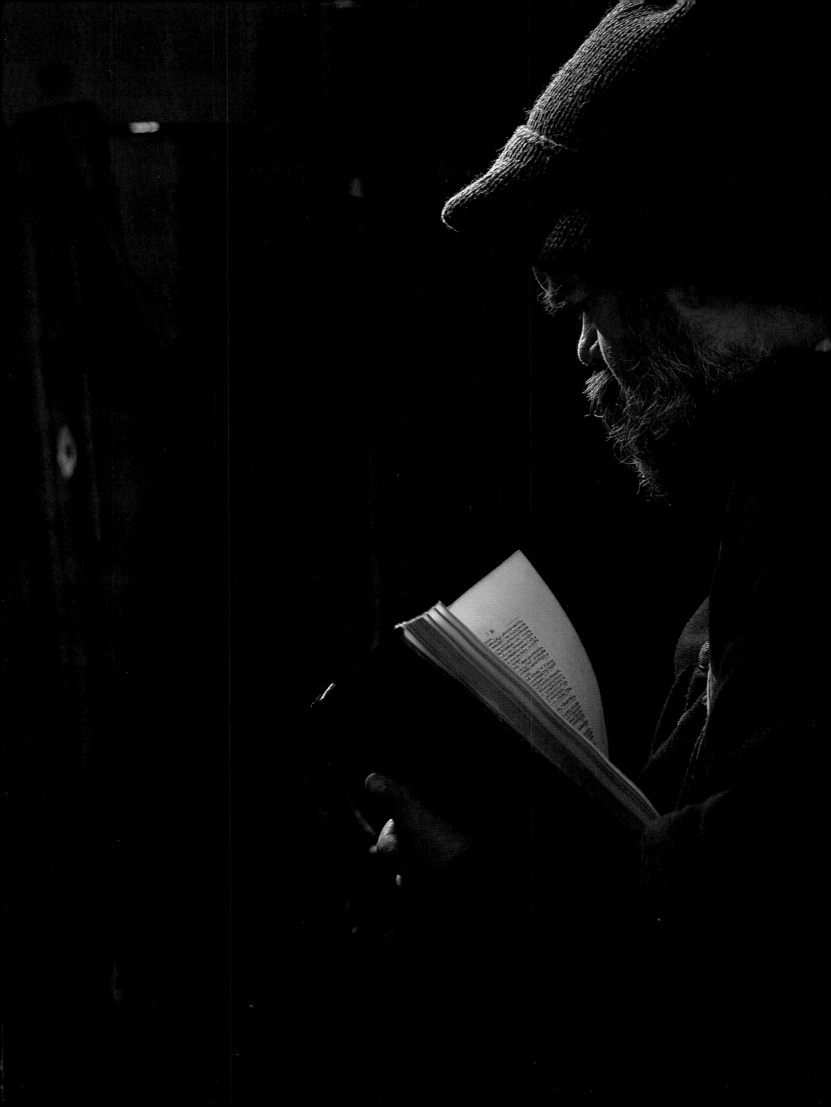

Prologue

THE PROPOSAL CAME FROM AN UNLIKELY SOURCE DURING THE DELIBERATIONS OF THE CONSTITUTIONAL CONVENTION IN PHILADELPHIA. BENJAMIN FRANKLIN WAS NOT KNOWN FOR HIS PIETY.

Born in Boston and reared a Calvinist, Franklin had migrated to Philadelphia, where he fashioned a remarkable career as an inventor, a printer, and a pundit. Franklin had long ago dispensed with the austere religion of his childhood in favor of Deism, the notion that God exists but chooses not to meddle in the day-to-day affairs of humanity. Deism, after all, was the religion most compatible with Enlightenment Rationalism, which elevated the notion of human reason over divine revelation. Its preferred approach was scientific inquiry rather than a leap of faith.

Although he befriended the likes of George Whitefield, the itinerant Anglican whose preaching had ignited the revival fires of the Great Awakening, Franklin remained suspicious of organized religion. Franklin admired Jesus, but he thought that those who identified themselves as the followers of Jesus too often emphasized piety at the expense of charity. "The faith you mention has doubtless, its use in the world," Franklin wrote to Whitefield in 1753. "I do not desire to see it diminished, nor would I desire to lessen it in any way; but I wish it were more productive of good works than I have generally seen it. I mean real good works, works of kindness, charity, mercy, and public spirit, not holy-day keeping, sermon-hearing, and reading, performing church ceremonies, or making long prayers, filled with flatteries and compliments, despised even by wise men, and much less capable of pleasing the Deity."[1]

Previous Page: The Puritans brought the Bible with them. Originally it was likely the Geneva Bible, but it was eventually replaced by the King James Version of the Bible, the official Bible of the American colonies.

Opposite: Benjamin Franklin and Patrick Henry were fellow delegates at the Constitutional Convention in 1787.

Courtesy of film First Freedom. Photographer, Mark Mabry. • Horace E. Scudder, A History of the United States of America (New York: Sheldon and Company, 1897), 36. Copyright © 2004–2012 Florida Center for Instructional Technology.

Franklin, the former minister to France for the new nation and a member of the Royal Society of Science, enjoyed the status of elder statesman during the deliberations of the Constitutional Convention. And when Franklin asked to speak during that sweltering summer of 1787, all eyes shifted to the venerable gentleman from Pennsylvania.

"I have lived, Sir, a long time," Franklin began, "and the longer I live, the more convincing proof I see of this truth—*that God governs in the affairs of men.* And if a sparrow cannot fall to the ground without his notice, is it probable that an empire can rise without his aid? Without his concurring we shall succeed in this political building no better than the Builders of Babel. And what is worse, mankind may hereafter

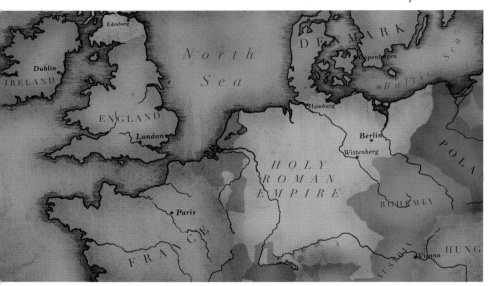

Entanglement between church and state began centuries ago with the conversion of Roman emperor Constantine to Christianity. The Holy Roman Empire, which extended over most of Europe from the tenth to the early nineteenth centuries, represented the apex of church-state entanglement in the West.

Map courtesy of Adam Hill.

from this unfortunate incident, despair of establishing governments by human wisdom and leave it to chance, war, and conquest."

The delegates waited to see where Franklin was headed with his remarks. "I therefore beg leave to move—that henceforth *prayers* imploring the assistance of Heaven, be held in this Assembly *every morning* before we proceed business."[2]

Even more remarkable than the provenance of this proposal, however, was the response. The delegates overwhelmingly rejected Franklin's proposal to begin each day's deliberations with prayer. At the bottom of his prepared remarks, the astonished Franklin appended the following notation: "The convention, except three or four persons, thought prayers unnecessary!"[3]

As the delegates met that summer in Philadelphia, nothing less was at stake than the contours of the new nation, and no issue was more vexing than configuration of church and state—religion and politics—in the fledgling United States of America. For centuries, especially in the West, the accepted wisdom was that church and state functioned as interlocking and mutually enforcing entities.

The conversion of the Roman emperor Constantine to Christianity following the Battle of Milvian Bridge in 312 CE transformed a minority, persecuted religion into the state church. Constantine took an active role in ecclesiastical affairs. He returned church property that had been confiscated during persecutions, convened church councils, and, because he retained his allegiance to the sun god, he moved the Christian day of worship from the Sabbath to the venerable day of the sun, Sunday.

Thus began centuries of entanglement between church and state. With the decline and fall of the Roman

Empire, the Roman Catholic Church effectively moved into the breach and assumed greater political powers. The Holy Roman Empire, which extended over most of Europe from the tenth to the early nineteenth centuries, represented the apex of church-state entanglement in the West. Strong popes, wielding the threat of excommunication, occasionally brought princes to their knees, while at other times—such as during the Avignon papacy in the fourteenth century—political rulers meddled shamelessly in the affairs of the church.

Conflict abounded. Martin Luther's theological assault on Rome divided Western Christianity and also spawned political divisions. The Wars of Religion in France pitted Catholics against Protestants, better known as Huguenots, in a series of conflicts from 1562 until the Edict of Nantes in 1598 brought a measure of toleration and several decades of peace.

In England, the context that would be most familiar to the delegates in Philadelphia, Parliament's Act of Supremacy of 1534, declared Henry VIII and his successors the "supreme head" of the Church of England because of the pope's refusal to annul his marriage to Catherine of Aragon. Henry was no fan of Martin Luther, whose Protestant Reformation had challenged the Roman Catholic Church and recast the religious and political landscape of the West, but his break with the papacy put

Martin Luther, father of the Protestant revolution, showed his displeasure with the dominant church by publicly burning the papal publication.

Courtesy Bridgeman Art Library, Martin Luther Burns the Papal Bull, circa nineteenth century; artist unknown.

King Henry VIII formed the Church of England when the Catholic Church refused his request for a divorce from his queen, Catherine of Aragon.

Courtesy Bridgeman Art Library, Henry VIII and Catherine of Aragon before the Papal Council, Frank O. Salisbury, 1910.

the Church of England on a generally Protestant course.

Though such was not without severe disruptions. Edward VI's regents pushed the Church of England in a more Protestant direction, but his successor, Mary I, better known as "Bloody Mary," had other ideas. Mary, Catherine of Aragon's daughter, sought to restore the Church of England to Rome and was willing to go to almost any lengths to do so. The architects of the Church of England—Hugh Latimer, Nicholas Ridley, and Thomas Cranmer—perished in the fires of Smithfield, while many other Protestants scattered to Europe to escape persecution. There, they settled in such Protestant cities as Frankfort, Strasbourg, and Geneva, where they observed Protestantism in full flower. With Mary's

death in 1558 and the conclusion of the Marian Exile, these Protestants returned to England eager to configure church and state along the lines they had witnessed on the Continent.

Elizabeth I, Mary's successor, refused to be bullied by the exiles newly returned from the Continent and impatient for reform. In part, she had to worry about the Spanish armada bobbing off the coast of France; too many concessions to Protestants might further provoke the Spaniards. Although a favorable July wind in the summer of 1588 allowed the English navy to defeat the armada and therefore permitted the Church of England to list a tad more toward Protestantism, Elizabeth was not interested in mimicking Geneva. She determinedly sought a *via media*—a middle way—for the Church of England between Roman Catholicism on the one hand and Protestantism on the other.

Both sides felt slighted by this configuration. Recusancy laws forced Catholics underground to practice their faith, sometimes quite literally in underground chapels and hiding places, while Protestants stepped up their efforts to purge the Church of England of all vestiges of Roman Catholicism. Thus was born Puritanism, the movement to "purify" the Church of England.

The tug of war between church and state in England continued into the seventeenth century. The transition from Tudor to Stuart monarchy brought more whipsaw moments for the faithful in England. James VI, coming down from Scotland to assume the throne as James I of England, excited Puritan hopes because Protestantism had already prevailed in Scotland in the form of the Presbyterian Church. On his way to Whitehall in 1603, James was intercepted by a group of Puritans and presented with the Millenary Petition, a list of reforms signed by a thousand members of the clergy. Although James rejected most of the proposals, he authorized one: a new English-language translation of the Bible. The Authorized Version, better known as the King James Version, appeared in 1611.

Charles I, his son, was even less disposed to the Puritans, in part because he had taken a Catholic wife, Henrietta Maria of France (the namesake of the American colony of Maryland).

The king had little interest in advancing the cause of the Puritans, and his appointment of William Laud, a virulent adversary of the Puritans, as chancellor of Oxford and, later, as archbishop of Canterbury, angered the Puritans.

In the midst of their declining fortunes at court, a small band of Puritans  led by John Winthrop despaired of ever reforming the Church of England and decided to show England and the world how church and state should be configured. But in order to do so, they would have to construct their "city on a hill" on the other side of the Atlantic.

King James appeased the Puritans of 1604 by agreeing to produce a new translaton of the Bible. In 1611, the King James Version of the Bible became the official Bible of the English realm and was quickly adopted by the faithful who emigrated to the American colonies.

Reenactment courtesy of Fires of Faith, Groberg Films and BYU TV. Photograph by Steve Porter.

"We are not a nation in the traditional sense. We have no ethnic base. We have no religious base. We have no racial base. To be an American is to believe in equality; liberty, and constitutionalism. Our founders created those ideals, that belief in democracy and the institutions by which we make that democracy work. And that's why we go back to them periodically—to reaffirm and refresh our sense of who we are. We don't take that for granted. That's why we study them so much. That's why we ask questions about them. Americans today want to know, 'What would Thomas Jefferson think of Affirmative Action?' 'What would George Washington say about the invasion of Iraq?' I don't know any other country that would ever ask those kinds of questions about the people in their past. Why do we do that? Because they created whatever sense of nationhood we have in these ideals, these aspirations, these beliefs. That's why we are so fascinated with these men." —Gordon Wood

Courtesy of film First Freedom. *Photographer, Mark Mabry.*

The delegates in Philadelphia were aware of this history of church-state relations. Perhaps they were weary of these entanglements. More likely, they had witnessed the success of more distant, less fraught relations between church and state in such colonies as Rhode Island, New York, and Pennsylvania. Perhaps it was time to seek a new paradigm, one utterly without precedent in Western history.

Benjamin Franklin's proposal for prayer at the beginning of each session went down to defeat. Despite the stifling heat in Philadelphia, the winds of change were blowing.

Religion and Liberty of Conscience

"Come, let us pray together," Benjamin Franklin said because of the enormity of what they were doing. They were in a particularly difficult moment. Interestingly, the Constitutional Convention said no and simply moved on. That upset Franklin, which you wouldn't expect given Franklin's live-and-let-live sensibility. The idea of *public religion*, which is a phrase of Franklin's from his 1749 syllabus for what became the University of Pennsylvania, is an important one, because the founders wanted to acknowledge and respect the role of religion but did not want to force it on the populous. That had already been done. It hadn't worked out very well and it had violated their sense of liberty of conscience. If one did not want to simply trade one form of tyranny for another, my sense is that particularly the very religiously devout founders understood that it's actually a religious position to be supportive of religious liberty. After all, if God Himself didn't compel obedience, but simply encouraged it, then no man should try. And that is the theological basis for religious liberty. Coercion is not belief, and it is the religious people who tend to best understand that. Roger Williams, the founder of Rhode Island, talked about how the wilderness of the world should not be allowed to contaminate the garden of Christ's church. There are those who saw the state as the threat to the church, not the church as the threat to the state.

JON MEACHAM

The growth of American churches in the eighteenth century can be illustrated by changes in city skylines over the course of the century. In New York City, an empty vista in 1690 had become a forest of eighteen steeples by 1771.

"Prospect of the City of New York" Woodcut from Hugh Gaine, New York Almanac, 1771. Library of Congress.

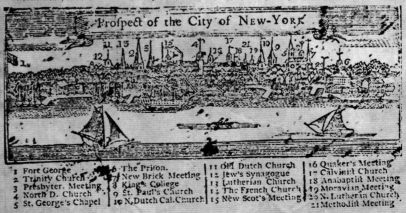

1

A City Upon A
HILL

Further know these are but
the beginnings of Christ's
glorious reformation and restoration
of his churches to a more
glorious splendor than ever.

— EDWARD JOHNSON —

Wonder-Working Providence of Sion's Savior
in New England (c. 1650)[4]

ALTHOUGH THE PURITANS OCCUPY A CENTRAL PLACE IN THE STORY OF AMERICAN ORIGINS, IT'S IMPORTANT TO REMEMBER THAT THEY WERE BY NO MEANS THE FIRST EUROPEAN SETTLERS IN THE NEW WORLD. The Spaniards preceded the Puritans by more than a century; Santa Fe, founded in 1610, is the oldest capital city in what is now the United States of America. The short-lived colony of Jamestown was founded in 1607, and the Pilgrims, who had already separated from the Church of England, arrived a decade before the Puritans and set up Plimouth Colony in 1620.

New Amsterdam was the Dutch West India Company's trading outpost in the New World, and the diversity of its earliest inhabitants prefigured the multicultural character that would become the hallmark of the region. Nearly a century after Giovanni da Verrazano, an Italian navigator in the service of France, discovered the inlet into New York harbor and the island we call Manhattan, Henry Hudson, an Englishman under contract to the Dutch East India Company, nosed the *Half Moon* through the same narrows and struggled north on the river that now bears his name. In addition to the Native Americans already here, New Netherland from its earliest days was notable for its racial, ethnic, and religious diversity.

Previous: William Brewster was the first minister in the new Massachusetts Bay Company at Salem, Massachusetts.

Right: On board the ship *Arbella*, John Winthrop gave his famous "City upon a Hill" speech to his fellow Puritan travelers.

The first group of settlers to disembark in Manhattan were Walloons, French-speaking Belgians, followed shortly by a modest influx of Dutch, Germans, and French. English Puritans eventually bracketed Dutch settlement on Long Island, while Swedes and Finns became the early denizens on the Delaware River to the south. Early reports filtering back to Amsterdam told of Huguenots, Mennonites, Brownists, Presbyterians, Quakers, Catholics, even "many atheists and various other servants of Baal."[5]

When Jonas Michaëlius, the first Dutch Reformed minister in New Netherland, convened the first religious gathering in New Amsterdam in 1628, he commented on the religious diversity already evident in the colony. "At the first administration of the Lord's Supper which was observed, not without great joy and comfort to many," he wrote to his superiors back in Amsterdam, "we had fully fifty communicants —Walloons and Dutch." In 1654 the *Sainte Catherine* pulled into port, carrying twenty-three Sephardic Jews, refugees from Recifé. Why did they choose New Amsterdam? The Netherlands was the most tolerant society in Europe in the seventeenth century, and that tradition of tolerance marked New Netherland as well.[6]

The small band of English Puritans, led by John Winthrop, would not be known for their toleration. Winthrop and others had despaired of ever reforming the Church of England according to the Protestant ideals they held dear. Their only option, they believed, was to migrate across the Atlantic and set up church and state in such a way that the two would be virtually indistinguishable. One entity

would support and reinforce the other, consistent with the pattern back in England.

And that, in fact, was precisely what they did. Winthrop and his fellow Puritans carried the charter for the Massachusetts Bay Company with them to the New World. This allowed them considerable latitude in shaping their society, and they did so consistent with their ideals, which Winthrop had expressed in a sermon aboard the *Arbella* during the Atlantic crossing. "For we must consider that we shall be as a city upon a hill," Winthrop preached. "The eyes of all people are upon us, so that if we shall deal falsely with our God in

Above: The mast of the *Mayflower II* at Plimoth Plantation in Plymouth, Massachusetts.

Next page: The Puritan colony at Plimoth Plantation in Plymouth, Massachusetts.
Photographer, Mark Mabry.

Above: Between April 8 and June 12, 1630, Puritan emigrants transported the Charter of the Massachusetts Bay Company from England to Salem, thereby giving legal birth to the Commonwealth of Massachusetts. John Winthrop, reputed to have given his famous "City upon a Hill" sermon aboard the ship, was elected governor of the Massachusetts Bay Colony twelve times.

Inset: The Reverend John Cotton (1585–1652)

Courtesy of film First Freedom. *Photographer, Mark Mabry. • First page of the Massachusetts Bay Colony Charter courtesy Boston Public Library, Charter, King William and Queen Mary, 1742. • This engraving, originally done in 1856 by H. W. Smith and copied from a painting that was in the possession of John R. Thayer at the time, was published in Samuel G. Drake,* The History and Antiquities of Boston *[1630 – 1770] (1856), 158.*

Puritan clergy, such as John Cotton, enjoyed both ecclesiastical power and political influence in Massachusetts, and they were expected, as ministers, to reinforce the social order. The meetinghouse, located on the "common," or the village green, was the religious, social, and political center of the community. Town meetings were conducted there, thereby signaling a unity of church and state that was more than symbolic.

Not everyone thought this configuration was a healthy one, and no one dissented more vociferously than Roger Williams. Educated at Cambridge University, the seedbed of Puritanism back in England, Williams migrated to New England in 1631 to become minister of the Puritan congregation at Salem. Very quickly, however, Williams became a critic of the way Massachusetts conducted its affairs. He predicted, correctly, that the Puritans would have trouble if they continued to encroach on Indian lands. More important, he quarreled with the Puritan fusion of church and state, pointing out that "the setting up of civil power and officers to judge the conviction of men's souls" was not only an absurdity, but was also at the root of civil and even military conflict ever since Constantine's conversion centuries earlier. "Where find you evidence of a whole nation, country or kingdom converted to the faith, and of Christ's appointing of a whole nation or kingdom to walk in one way of religion?" Williams asked.[9]

this work we have undertaken, and so cause him to withdraw his present help from us, we shall be made a story and a by-word through the world."[7]

Massachusetts was configured in such a way that only landholding church members had the right to vote. "Theocracy, or to make the Lord God our governor, is the best form of government in a Christian commonwealth," John Cotton wrote in his *Discourse about Civil Government*. In that commonwealth, Cotton continued, "the power of civil administration is denied unto unbelievers" and the task of governing is "committed to the saints."[8]

In a memorable metaphor that would be picked up by Thomas Jefferson nearly two centuries later, Williams wanted to segregate the "garden of the church" from the "wilderness of the world" by means of a "hedge or wall of separation." Those images have become so familiar that they may have lost some of their meaning, and to understand the significance of that metaphor we must recall that the Puritans did not share our idyllic, post-Thoreau romantic notions about wilderness. For the Puritans of the seventeenth century, struggling to carve a godly society out of the howling wilderness of Massachusetts, *wilderness* was a place of danger. It was a place of darkness where evil lurked. So when Williams wanted to protect the "garden" of the church from the "wilderness" of the world, he was concerned to preserve the integrity of the church from defilement by too close an association with the state.[10]

Other Puritans, however, harbored no worries whatsoever about such a conflation of church and state; in fact, such collusion was the entire reason for migrating to the New World. In October 1635, Williams was haled into the General Court of Massachusetts, convicted of heresy and sedition, and was banished from the colony. The judgment against him declared that he had been spreading "diverse new & dangerous opinions." In January 1636, Williams fled Salem on foot

for Narragansett Bay, where he eventually established Providence, after having purchased land from the Indians.[11]

Although the Puritans came to regard it as a kind of cesspool of religious heresy, Williams envisioned his new settlement as a haven for those "distressed of conscience." The charter itself, finally granted by Charles II in 1663, referred to Rhode Island as a "lively experiment" where it might be proved that "a flourishing civil state may best be maintained among his Majesty's subjects with full religious liberty." The charter further stipulated that "no person within the said colony shall hereafter be any wise molested or called in question for any difference in opinion in matters of religion that does not disturb the civil peace of the colony."[12]

Williams himself took full advantage of his haven of tolerance. In 1639 Ezekiel Holliman baptized Williams by immersion; Williams in turn baptized Holliman and ten others, thereby marking the beginning of the Baptist tradition in America. Ever since, with some notable lapses, the Baptist tradition has been defined by two tenets: adult (or believer's) baptism and liberty of conscience, embodied in part by the separation of church and state.

Another Puritan who ran afoul of the authorities in Massachusetts was Anne Hutchinson, who had migrated to the New World with her pastor, John Cotton. Hutchinson soon began

THE
CHARTER
Granted by their Majesties
King WILLIAM
AND
Queen MARY,
TO THE
INHABITANTS
OF THE
PROVINCE
OF THE
Maſſachuſetts-Bay
IN
NEW-ENGLAND.

BOSTON, in NEW-ENGLAND:
Printed by S. KNEELAND, by Order of His Excellency the
GOVERNOR, COUNCIL and House of REPRESENTATIVES.
M,DCC,LIX.

Roger Williams was an outspoken advocate of religious freedom and was one of the first challengers of Puritan theocracy. Williams was banished from the Massachusetts Bay Colony for his toleration and support for religious diversity, which included "Jews, Pagans, and Turks." His defiance over state control of religious freedom led to his expulsion from the state. He moved to Rhode Island, where he founded the city of Providence. In 1644, Williams wrote a book on religious freedom, democracy, and intellectual freedom, *The Bloody Tenent of Persecution.*

Roger Williams portrait taken from George J. Hagar, The Standard American Encyclopedia.

Above: In the colony, the villagers were called to worship by the sound of a drum.

Courtesy of film First Freedom. *Photographer, Mark Mabry.*

Right: Both the church and the courthouse were found in the same structure on the Plimoth Plantation. Puritan parishioners expressed their worship in several forms, but were intolerant of other faiths.

Courtesy of film First Freedom. *Photographer, Mark Mabry.*

criticizing John Wilson and other ministers for deviating from Puritan orthodoxy in their preaching about the role of good works in securing salvation. Even more brazenly, Hutchinson convened groups of women for the purposes of engaging in such conversations. Puritan authorities found her actions doubly subversive: Not only was a lay person challenging the theological integrity of the clergy, a woman was challenging the authority of men.

Hutchinson's turn in court, charged with "traducing the ministers," came in September 1637. For much of the proceedings, Hutchinson parried her accusers to a draw. But the fix was in; Hutchinson's insubordination would not go unpunished. In a summation reminiscent of Martin Luther at the Imperial Diet of Worms a century earlier, Hutchinson declared, "You have no power over my body, neither can you do me any harme, for I am in the hands of the eternall Jehovah my Saviour, I am at his appointment, the bounds of my habitation are cast in heaven, no further doe I esteeme of any mortal man than creatures in his hand." The defendant, who was probably pregnant at the time, steadied herself and continued. "I feare none but the great Jehovah, which hath foretold me of these things, and I doe verily beleeve that he will deliver me out of our hands, therefore take heed how you proceed against me; for I know that for this you goe about to doe to me, God will ruine you and your posterity, and this whole State."[13]

Judgment was swift and unequivocal. "Forasmuch as you, Mrs. Hutchinson, have highly transgressed and offended," and in "so many ways troubled the Church with your errors,"

John Winthrop declared, "I do not only pronounce you worthy to be cast out, but I do cast you out, and in the name of Christ I do deliver you up to Satan that you may learn no more to blaspheme, to seduce, and to lie."[14]

As with Roger Williams, Anne Hutchinson's treatment at the hands of the Puritans confirmed that Massachusetts would not tolerate liberty of conscience or challenges to the authority of either church or state. After spending some time in Rhode Island, Williams's

A Model of CHRISTIAN CHARITY

John Winthrop's "City Upon a Hill" Analogy

******** 🏛 *******

John Winthrop's speech is a remarkably profound, theologically deep statement—it moves between both theoretical and theological sophistication to very practical implications: how people should treat each other and how they should take care of their economic straits in the wilderness they would be facing. And then it finishes with this very powerful image of America (New England at the time) "as a city upon a hill." Winthrop's vision was that if we would live this principle—if we would truly practice Christian charity with one another in both the internal mechanisms of our heart, where we really felt it, and would really put it into practice—that America would become a "city upon a hill." That's exactly what has happened. This image has cascaded down through our American political tradition. It is a motif that is often associated with Ronald Reagan, and the speech in general has been alluded to and embraced by presidents all the way from John Adams to Bill Clinton. John Winthrop's notion is that America has a special role to play in the world—that it can be an exemplary nation. But of course this vision is grounded on a certain sort of moral outlook: that America will be exemplary because we treat people in a certain way, in an ethical way, in a caring and genuine way that will allow us to play this role. So Winthrop's speech had a big impact in his day. It has continued to speak to us down through the ages, such that at the turn of the millennium some have called it the greatest sermon of the last thousand years. That is quite a statement, but it is generally now acknowledged to stand at the beginning of our political civic consciousness.

—·······—

MATTHEW S. HOLLAND

haven of toleration, Hutchinson migrated to Long Island, where in 1643 she and her family, except for one daughter, were killed by Indians. The Hutchinson River (and the Hutchinson River Parkway) is named in her honor.

⁂

Religious minorities fared somewhat better in other colonies. Although Pieter Stuyvesant, director-general of New Netherland for the Dutch West India Company, tried to secure established status for the Dutch Reformed Church, the colony's rampant pluralism rendered that task nearly impossible. Stuyvesant had resisted the immi-

gration of Jews who came aboard the *Sainte Catherine* in 1654, and he sought to thwart the Quakers in Flushing. In response, thirty-one of the residents of Flushing, none of them Quakers, protested the director-general's action on December 27, 1657. "The law of loue, peace and libertie in the states extending to *Jewes*, *Turkes* and *Egiptians*, as they are Considered sonnes of Adam, which is the glory of the outward State of *Holland*, soe loue, peace and libertie extending to all in Christ Jesus, Condemns hatred, warre, and bondage," the Flushing Remonstrance read. The statement, one of the earliest expressions of religious toleration in American history, concluded with a

remarkable plea for inclusiveness: "Our desire is not to offend one of his little ones, in what soever forme, name or title hee appeares in, whether presbiterian, independant, Baptist or Quaker, but shall bee glad to see any thing of god in any of them: desireing to doe vnto all men as wee desire all men shoulde doe vnto vs, which is the true law both of Church and State. For our Saviour saith this is the Law and the Prophets."[15]

Stuyvesant queried his superiors back in the Netherlands for guidance about how to deal with the colony's burgeoning diversity, especially the Quakers. They responded that "although we heartily desire, that these and other sectarians remained away from there, yet as they do not, we doubt very much, whether we can proceed against them rigorously without diminishing the population and stopping immigration." The directors of the West India Company were prepared to pursue a pragmatic course. "You may therefore shut your eyes," they told Stuyvesant, "at least not force the people's consciences, but allow every one to have his own belief, as long as he behaves quietly and legally, gives no offence to his neighbors and does not oppose the government."[16]

Although Maryland had been founded by Roman Catholics from England, Richard Ingle, a ship captain and a Protestant, navigated his vessel, the *Reformation*, to St. Mary's in 1645 and laid siege to the colony's capital. Acting, he insisted, on behalf of the new Puritan government back in England, Ingle detained the colony's leaders and took two Jesuits back to England in chains. This revolt of Protestants, called Ingle's Rebellion, marginalized Catholics in the colony, although the Toleration Act, passed by the Maryland Assembly in

Pieter Stuyvesant, Director-General of New Netherland

Unknown painter (attributed to Hendrick Couturier; in the past was considered a Rembrandt), ca. 1660, New York Historical Society. Public domain due to copyright expiration.

A LAW OF MARYLAND Concerning RELIGION.

Above: Large broadside on the Maryland Toleration Act.

Images of American Political History, public domain in the United States.

Opposite: Anne Hutchinson was banished from the Puritan colony for sedition; she taught religion in her home and criticized the local clergy. She was pregnant with her fifteenth child when she was put on trial in 1637 and subsequently banished from the colony.

Courtesy of film First Freedom. Photographer, Mark Mabry.

"You couldn't enter New York as a Catholic. It was against the law. . . . There were no Catholic Churches in New York or in Massachusetts. It simply was not tolerated. They weren't even seen by some as Christians—they were called heathens. But then, the Catholics called the Protestants heathens. The Quakers were seen as Atheists by the Church of England and by other groups." —Patricia Bonomi

Ferd. Mayer & Sons Liths., courtesy Library of Congress.

1649, returned a measure of religious liberty by once again extending toleration to all Christians. A new government in 1654, however, mandated that "none who profess and Exercise the Popish Religion Commonly known by the Name of the Roman Catholick Religion can be protected in this Province."[17]

A more successful venture in religious toleration unfolded next door in Pennsylvania. The king of England owed William Penn's family more than

£16,000 in back wages for his father's labors, so the son struck a deal with the crown: To satisfy the debt, the king granted William Penn a charter for a colony in America. Penn saw this as a way to act on his Quaker beliefs in equality, toleration, and pacifism. His "Holy Experiment," begun in 1682, offered the right to own property, the right to trial by jury, and the ability to engage in commerce with few restrictions. Penn, like Roger Williams before him, maintained good relations with the Native Americans in the area. In his *Concessions to the Province of Pennsylvania,* Penn mandated that "no man shall, by any ways or means, in word, or deed, affront, or wrong any Indian," and the preface to Pennsylvania's *Frame of Government* in 1682 envisioned a government "capable of kindness, goodness, and charity." Penn himself learned the languages of the Shawnee, the Susquehannock, and the Leni-Lanape Indians.

At the center of Penn's vision was religious toleration, and throughout the colonial period various religious groups, persecuted elsewhere, found shelter in Pennsylvania. The list includes Quakers, Lutherans, Mennonites, and the Amish, followers of Jakob Amman.

Many Roman Catholics sought refuge in Penn's "Holy Experiment." On September 22, 1734, the *St. Andrew* sailed into Philadelphia carrying forty families of Schwenckfelders, followers of the Silesian Protestant reformer Caspar Schwenckfeld von Ossig, a group that had been persecuted by both Protestants and Catholics in Europe. A band of Moravians also migrated to Pennsylvania and founded a settlement along the Lehigh River on Christmas Eve, 1741; they called it Bethlehem.

NEW YORK.

The Contribution of the Puritans

The Puritans were the first in our history to establish and promote the idea that America was discovered and founded for a divine purpose. And with that thinking came the idea that somewhere in the center of our country would be New Jerusalem. They also felt that they were establishing a new Zion and that is the reason that they named it New England. They wanted to create an entirely new country, but they also wanted to have control of their religious practices. They did not come over here to offer religious freedom for people. They came here with the idea of having control. They saw the contention and the challenge that they had in England—so they wanted to have the control here so they could perhaps control their destiny and bring about the Zion and the New Jerusalem in which they themselves believed.

When considering the Puritans' influence in the early beginning of our country they really are important, because it was through their effort that we had an educated people. In their desire to control their situation, they developed thinkers—people who were diligently seeking truth—because they wanted every individual to be educated. That was the foundation of our country. And from that came the dismantling of the Puritan movement as we saw opportunities for other religions to survive and to become part of the beginning fabric of this country.

————

CHARLES ALLEN

————

✶ ✶ ✶ ✶ ✶ ✶ ✶ ✶ ✶ ✶ ✶ ✶ ✶ ✶ ✶ ✶ ✶ ✶

The hard-won religious toleration in New Netherland suffered a blow when political control of the colony fell to the English in the English Conquest of 1664. The colony reverted briefly to the Dutch in 1673, but the follow-

Cornbury's detractors accused him of dressing as a woman (purportedly to emphasize his physical resemblance to his cousin, Queen Anne) and parading on the ramparts of the fort and through the streets of New York. Whether or not

ing year the Treaty of Westminster ceded the colony finally to the English and renamed it in honor of the Duke of York. The Duke's Laws ostensibly guaranteed freedom of religion, but a succession of English governors sought to prefer the Church of England over all others. Benjamin Fletcher pressured the assembly to pass the Ministry Act of 1693, which provided tax monies to support Anglicanism in the colony, but the Dutch Reformed ministers found ingenious ways to frustrate implementation of the scheme.

Edward Hyde, Viscount Cornbury, who assumed the office of governor in 1701, was even more tenacious.

he actually did so, the governor was tireless in his efforts to promote Anglicanism in the colony. Several years into his tenure as governor, Cornbury promised the Society for the Propagation of the Gospel, the missionary arm of the Church of England, that "nothing shall be wanting on my part to promote" the society's "good and pious designs." On Long Island, Cornbury had replaced dissenting ministers with Anglican clergy, and he appointed Anglican ministers to serve in Dutch Reformed churches. "Now I am of Opinion that if as ye Dutch Ministers dye, those Churches were supply'd with English ministers," Cornbury wrote back

An early champion of democracy and religious freedom, William Penn founded Pennsylvania as a haven for those practicing religious toleration. He was also successful in forging a number of treaties with the Lenape Indians.

William Penn's Treaty with the Indians, John Boydell, 1775, courtesy Library of Congress.

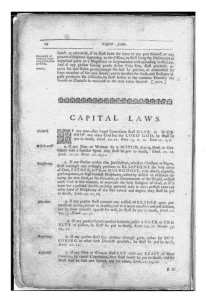

Above: *The Book of General Lawes for Massachusetts* lists witchcraft, the second law in the book, as a crime punishable by death.

Above Right: Mary Dyer being led to the gallows on Boston Common, where she was executed. Most of the murdered "witches" were women.

Right: Cotton Mather's 1693 book, *The Wonders of the Invisible World,* provides a detailed justification for the Salem witch trials, explaining how the world is populated by "Spectral Representations." For Mather, "Spectral Exhibitions" were the work of violent, diabolical spirits from another realm; nevertheless, most of the murdered "witches" were mortal women.

Opposite: Young children were kept away from the trials of accused witches to shelter them from the "evil" of the accused.

The Book of the General Lawes and Libertyes Concerning the Inhabitants of the Massachusets (1648; facsimile edition, Cambridge: Harvard University Press, 1929). • The Quaker Mary Dyer led to execution on Boston Common, 1 June 1660, by unknown nineteenth-century artist. Courtesy Brooklyn Museum. This is a faithful photographic reproduction of an original two-dimensional work of art; the art itself is in the public domain because its copyright has expired. This applies to Australia, the European Union, and those countries with a copyright term of life of the author plus 70 years. • Title page from Cotton Mather, The Wonders of the Invisible World, 1693. Courtesy Sunderland Libraries • Courtesy of film First Freedom. Photographer, Mark Mabry.

to London in 1705, "that would with schools be a means to make this Colony and English Colony which I am afraid will not easily be done without it."[18]

To the north, in New England, the Puritan quest to meld church and state, religion and politics, turned violent. Quaker missionaries began arriving in the colony to convert Puritans to the Society of Friends. But Puritan leaders, both civil and ecclesiastical, were not amused, especially because the Quakers taught that the "inner light" was available to all people, including women. Quakers were thrown in jail, and some had their ears cropped or their tongues burned for speaking such heresy. Most were exiled from the colony with a stern warning not to return, on pain of execution. But return they did. Between the years 1659 and 1661, four Quakers were hanged on Boston Common. In the course of her trial, and just after being sentenced to death, Mary Dyer made an eloquent appeal for religious toleration.

She enjoined her accusers to "Repeal all such Laws, that the Truth and Servants of the Lord may have free Passage among you, and be kept from shedding Innocent Blood."[19]

Mary Dyer's appeal for religious toleration fell on deaf ears. On June 1, 1660, at the gallows on Boston Common, Dyer was given one final opportunity to renounce her beliefs and thereby choose exile rather than execution. She refused.

The Wonders of the Invisible World:

Being an Account of the

TRYAL

OF

Several Witches,

Lately Executed in

NEW-ENGLAND

And of several remarkable Curiosties therein Occurring

Together with,

I. Observations upon the Nature, the Number, and the Operations of the Devils.

II. A short Narrative of a late outrage committed by a knot of Witches in *Swede-Land,* very much resembling, and so far explaining, that under which *New-England* has laboured.

III. Some Councels directing a due Improvement of the Terrible things lately done by the unusual and amazing Range of Evil Spirits in *New-England.*

IV. A brief Discourse upon those *Temptations* which are the more ordinary Devices of Satan.

By COTTON MATHER.

Published by the Special Command of his EXCELLENCY the Governour of the Province of the *Massachusetts-Bay* in New-England.

Printed first, at *Boston* in *New-England;* and Reprinted at *London,* for *John Dunton,* at the *Raven* in the *Poultry.* 1693.

3

The Making of
RELIGIOUS
POPULISM

Several told me, that tho' they had liv'd **thirty**
forty *or* **fifty Years** *under the Preaching of*
the Gospel, they had never felt the Power of
the Word upon their Hearts, so as to be long
affected thereby, at any Time as they did then.

— JONATHAN PARSONS —

"Account of the Revival at Lyme" (1744) [20]

Previous page: George Whitefield giving one of many sermons across the colonies, circa 1740.

Above: An accused "witch" being tried in Salem.

Courtesy of film First Freedom. Photographer, Mark Mabry. • Courtesy Bridgeman Art Library, Examination of a Witch, 1853, oil on canvas, Tompkins, Harrison, Matteson.

B Y THE TURN OF THE EIGHTEENTH CENTURY, RELIGION IN AMERICA HAD SETTLED INTO PATTERNS THAT, IF NOT ENTIRELY PREDICTABLE, TENDED TOWARD ROUTINE. Although there were periodic outbreaks of religious interest and enthusiasm—under the ministrations of Solomon Stoddard in the Connecticut Valley, for instance, or Guliam Bertholf in northern New Jersey—religious life among the colonists was remarkably quiescent. In New England, the great Puritan experiment of uniting church and state and establishing a city upon a hill had largely run its course by 1700, enervated by factionalism, by the professionalism of the clergy, and by interest in commerce, exemplified by the rise of the merchant class late in the seventeenth century. The Salem witch hysteria of 1692 persuaded many New Englanders that Satan was active in Massachusetts, the very heart of Puritanism. "Are not Gods *Sabbaths* woefully neglected?" Samuel Willard lamented in 1700. In New York, the eagerness of the Dutch Reformed clergy to ingratiate themselves to the new English rulers in the colony led to a disaffection of lower-class Dutch, evident most clearly in Leisler's Rebellion of 1689.[21]

A couple of decades into the eighteenth century, however, things began to change. In 1720, a young Dutch minister, Theodorus Jacobus Frelinghuysen, stepped off the vessel *King George* in New York City on his way to assume pastoral leadership of the Dutch Reformed congregations in the Raritan Valley of New Jersey. The boat's captain, Jacob Goelet, reported that the young minister had "condemned most of the preachers in Holland as not regenerated men." Before heading south to New Jersey, Frelinghuysen lodged with one of the Dutch ministers in New York City and criticized him for the vanity of having a mirror in his home and for using the Lord's Prayer—a formal rather than a spontaneous prayer—in his church services. When he arrived to assume leadership of his congregations, Frelinghuysen quickly denied Holy Communion to the more affluent members of his churches, charging that they did not possess the requisite piety to be true Christians.[22]

Frelinghuysen had been steeped in Pietism back in Europe. Pietism, a religious movement, was a reaction to the cold formalism and arid scholasticism that had been characteristic of much religious life in the seventeenth century. Pietists emphasized that true religion extended beyond mere intellectual assent; it must incorporate a warm-hearted, and often demonstrative, piety. This pietistic impulse took many forms, and it also crossed denominational and even religious boundaries: Methodism in the Church of England, for example, Quietism among Roman Catholics, and even Hasidism among the Jews.

When he arrived in New Jersey, Frelinghuysen skillfully rekindled class resentments that had been smoldering since Leisler's Rebellion, commenting that "the largest portion of the faithful have been poor and of little account in the world." He also preached about the need for a warm-hearted religion; faithful to his roots in Pietism, Frelinghuysen encouraged his congregants to cultivate religious affections.[23]

Several hundred miles to the north, another preacher, Jonathan Edwards, witnessed an outbreak of religious interest in Northampton, Massachusetts, during the winter of 1734–1735. The people of Northampton suddenly were convulsed with religious excitement, a condition that Edwards ascribed to a "surprising work of God." As with all religious enthusiasm, the fervor abated, but the arrival of an Anglican preacher, George Whitefield, again stirred religious sentiments. Trained in the London theater, Whitefield had mastered the art of grand gestures and dramatic pauses. His stentorian voice reverberated in churches, in

town squares, and even in the open air when the crowds grew too large or when he was denied access to other venues.

Whitefield appealed to the masses. With his emphasis on extemporary preaching, he rejected the formal style of many preachers and also their emphasis on difficult or esoteric theology. And in a culture with no theatrical tradition, Whitefield's command of thespian techniques overwhelmed many of the colonists. Contemporaries claimed that he could bring tears to your eyes simply by saying "Mesopotamia."

Colonists were intrigued. "I felt the Spirit of God drawing me by conviction," Nathan Cole of Farmington, Connecticut, recounted. Upon learning that Whitefield was preaching in

Top: Salem witch trial in progress, marked by fainting, accusing, and finger pointing.

Bottom Left: New York councilors Nicholas Bayard, Stephanus van Cortlandt, and Frederick Phillipse attempting to quiet revolutionary fears at the time of Leisler's Rebellion in New York City in 1689, when the royal governor, James II, was deposed because he was Catholic.

Bottom Right: Jonathan Edwards, 1703–1758, one of America's great philosophers and theologians.

Art by Alfred Fredericks; engraving by Albert Bobbett. NYPL digital gallery, public domain in the United States. • Engraved by R Babson & J Andrews; print by Wilson & Daniels, The History of Connecticut, from the First Settlement of the Colony to the Adoption of the Present Constitution, 1 New Haven, CT: Durrie and Peck. Public domain because its copyright has expired. This applies to those countries with a copyright term of life of the author plus 70 years.

GEORGE WHITEFIELD:
Phenomenon of the Colonief

George Whitfield was a man of amazing charisma and force, and as one study has suggested, he was trained as an actor at Oxford and had tremendous power over crowds. How else without amplification could he speak to 20,000 people with clarity? This is one of the things that Benjamin Franklin found fascinating. In Philadelphia, Benjamin Franklin would walk around and note the crowd's reaction—tens of thousands of people listening to Whitefield. But Whitefield was a radical in certain ways in denouncing conventional faith. He was an Evangelical in saying that if religion didn't cut deeply, if it didn't move people powerfully, then it was no good. So he would thumb his nose at the clergy—say they were too conventional, they were too dry, they were dead, and he would call people to repentance. He would do it outside ecclesiastical contexts, often with the opposition of the relevant Presbyterian, Congregational, Anglican clergy. But his message took hold and there were huge followings by people who encountered a form of Christianity that they could relate to—a form of Christianity they may not have found in their conventional churches.

Courtesy Bridgeman Art Library, "George Whitefield," illustration from H.D.M. Spence-Jones, The Church of England: A History for the People.

NATHAN O. HATCH

Middletown, Cole and his wife hurried to the scene, "and when we got to Middletown old meeting house there was a great Multitude it was said to be 3 or 4,000 of people Assembled together," Cole wrote. "When I saw Mr Whitefield, come upon the Scaffold he lookt almost angelical; a young, Slim, slender, Youth before some thousands of people with a bold undaunted Countenance, and my hearing how God was with him every where as he came along it Solemnized my mind, and put me into a trembling fear before he began to preach." Cole was persuaded by Whitefield's preaching: "And my hearing him preach, gave me a heart wound." Cole, thirty years old, recorded that he was "born again" on that occasion in October 1741.[24]

Whitefield's oratory was persuasive even to those not disposed toward his message. Although Benjamin Franklin had befriended Whitefield and admired him, Franklin was no fan of organized religion, and though he thought Whitefield's pet project, an orphanage in Georgia, was a worthy cause, Franklin believed that it would have been more useful had it been located in a larger city like Philadelphia. Despite his doubts, however, Franklin's account of Whitefield's visit to Society Hill in Philadelphia provides eloquent testimony to the power of Whitefield's oratory.

Franklin opened the narrative by calculating the size of the crowd that had gathered to hear the preacher— as many as ten thousand, according to Franklin's estimates. Franklin, milling through the crowd and listening to Whitefield, quickly determined that the preacher was ramping up toward an appeal for funds for his orphanage. "I silently resolved he should get nothing from me," Franklin recalled. "I had in my pocket a handful of copper money, three or four silver dollars and five pistoles in gold. As he proceeded I began to soften and concluded to give the coppers. Another stroke of his oratory made me ashamed of that, and determined me to give the silver. And he finished so admirably that I emptied my pockets wholly into the collection plate, gold and all."[25]

Even the redoubtable Franklin was not impervious to Whitefield's charms. As a postscript to his own response to Whitefield's preaching, Franklin told of an acquaintance, a Quaker, who had taken the precaution of emptying his pockets before coming to Society Hill, well aware of Whitefield's persuasive powers. By the conclusion of Whitefield's oration, this man, "Friend Hopkinson," was asking another man for a loan so that he could contribute to Whitefield's orphanage.

Whitefield inspired a legion of itinerant preachers—men like Gilbert Tennent, James Davenport, Eleazar Wheelock, Andrew Croswell, and many others—who crisscrossed the colonies with their message of spiritual renewal. Colonists flocked to hear these evangelical preachers, demanding more and more preaching. "Sab-

baths alone wou'd not suffice for hearing Sermons, but greater Numbers still urg'd for frequent Lectures," Jonathan Parsons reported from Connecticut. "I readily consented, upon the Request of the People, to preach as often as I cou'd, besides the stated Exercises of the Sabbath. "Together, these itinerant preachers served as catalysts for what contemporaries called "a great and general awakening," a movement historians refer to simply as the Great Awakening.[26]

One notable convert during the Great Awakening was Isaac Backus. Following his evangelical conversion in

Opposite: A wigged George Whitefield preaching in the open on a platform in Philadelphia.

Left: Moved by Whitefield's oratory, Benjamin Franklin donated generously to the plate when it was passed.

Above: Benjamin Franklin was a compendium of American intellectual interests—an auto-didact who would go on to chart the Gulf Stream and invent the lightning rod, bifocals, and the Franklin stove. He was a deeply unconventional man: He believed in God, but rejected organized religion.

Courtesy Bridgeman Art Library, Whitefield Preaching in Moorfields, *illustration by Eyre Crowe from H.D.M. Spence-Jones,* The Church of England: A History for the People, *pub. c. 1910. • Courtesy of film* First Freedom. *Photographer, Mark Mabry. • Courtesy Library of Congress,* D. Benjamin Franklin, *et vita inter Americanos, 1780.*

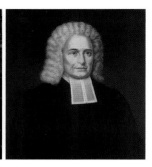

Though their physical appearance is similar, these preachers had very different techniques and opinions. Left to right:

Isaac Backus was a leading Baptist preacher during the Colonial period and was a proponent of separation of church and state.

Gilbert Tennent. A son of William Tennent, the founder of the Log College, Irish-born Gilbert Tennent played an influential role in the spread of Presbyterianism during the Great Awakening in the British colonies prior to his death in 1764.

Eleazar Wheelock, founder and first president of Dartmouth College in Hanover, New Hampshire.

Samuel Davies (1723–1761) was the spearhead of the efforts of New Side Presbyterians to evangelize Virginia and the South. Establishing himself in Hanover County, Virginia, in the 1740s, Davies was so successful in converting members of the Church of England to the new birth that he was soon embroiled in disputes with local officials about his right to preach the gospel where he chose.

Inset: A famous sermon preached by Gilbert Tennent at Nottingham, Pennsylvania, in 1740.

1741, Backus became a Baptist, thereby forsaking the Congregationalism that had enjoyed state sanction—and nearly hegemonic status—in New England. After serving as pastor of a Separate (not sanctioned by the state) congregation in Titicut, Massachusetts, Backus further defied the authorities by forming a Baptist congregation in Middleborough, Massachusetts, in 1756, where he served as pastor until his death half a century later. In 1764, Backus joined with other Baptists, including John and Nicholas Brown, as one of the original trustees of what became Brown University.

Baptists, like others the state of Massachusetts deemed "dissenters," were forced to support the Congregationalist establishment with their taxes, even though they did not worship in the Congregationalist Church. Those who refused to pay the taxes faced distraint of goods and property, even prison. Backus vigorously protested this, both through his preaching and his writing. As the American Revolution

THE
DANGER
OF
An Unconverted
MINISTRY,
Considered in a
SERMON
On MARK VI. 34.

Preached at *Nottingham*, in *Pennsylvania*, *March* 8. ANNO 1739,40.

By GILBERT TENNENT, A.M. And Minister of the Gospel in *New-Brunswick, New-Jersey*.

Jerem. V. 30, 31. *A wonderful and horrible Thing is committed in the Land: The Prophets prophesy falsely, and the Priests bear Rule by their Means, and my People love to have it so; and what will they do in the End thereof?*

PHILADELPHIA:
Printed by BENJAMIN FRANKLIN, In *Market-street*, 1740.

approached, Backus stepped up his calls for religious liberty. In 1773, for example, he preached a sermon calling for the separation of church and state, a sermon later published as *An Appeal to the Public for Religious Liberty, Against the Oppressions of the Present Day.* Noting the colonists' umbrage because of their oppression at the hands of Parliament by measures such as the Stamp Act, Backus challenged the authorities in Massachusetts to attend to the unfair taxation of religious dissenters closer to home. "God alone is Lord of the conscience," Backus wrote, adding that "our greatest difficulty at present concerns the submitting to a taxing power in ecclesiastical affairs."[27]

The Awakening had other effects beyond the emphasis on persuasive oratory and the clamor for religious liberty. Whitefield and other itinerants represented a populist challenge to both the social order and to other ministers, also known as the "settled clergy." In the early days of the revival, these ministers frequently would lend their pulpits to itinerant preachers, but they grew wary as they realized that the itinerants became increasingly critical of the settled clergy for their stodginess, their obsession with professionalism, and their lack of warm-hearted piety. A group of fourteen ministers in the Boston area, for example, issued a statement declaring their intention not to invite James Davenport "into our Places of publick worship." The clergy thought it their responsibility to shield their congregants from the itinerant and "to bear a Testimony against all those Disorders and that Prophaneness which have been promoted by any who have lately gone forth to hear him."[28]

The settled clergy had reason to be wary. On March 8, 1740, for example, Gilbert Tennent preached a sermon in Nottingham, Pennsylvania, called "The Danger of an Unconverted Ministry," an attack on ministers who, in Tennent's judgment, did not possess the requisite evangelical piety to serve as trustworthy spiritual guides. Sitting under such preaching, Tennent declared, rendered the auditors "as blind as Moles, and as dead as Stones, without any spiritual Taste and Relish." Tennent's sermon, which called on congregants to leave their churches and affiliate with revivalist preachers and congregations, was published and enjoyed wide circulation, especially in the middle colonies.

The settled clergy could often count on the civil authorities to defend their prerogatives against the itinerants. In Connecticut, for example, Davenport was brought before the general assembly in 1742. The legislators determined that "the behavior, conduct and doctrines advanced and taught by the said *James Davenport* do and have a natural

tendency to disturb and destroy the peace and order of this government." Davenport was deported by ferry from Connecticut across the Long Island Sound to Southold, New York.

As these itinerant preachers circulated along the Atlantic seaboard, they carried news of the revival in other colonies, thereby establishing networks of communication that would be essential to making a unified people out of

John Wesley, 1703–1791, was a cofounder of the Methodist movement and was an open air preacher, much like George Whitefield.

John Wesley Preaching, *Currier & Ives*, *courtesy of Library of Congress.*

Americanſ Slowly Learned *the* Value *of* RELIGIOUS DIVERSITY

The people of the New England colonies came out of a very strong Puritan Protestant reformation tradition that they brought from Europe. They also brought with them from Britain a strong antipathy to Catholicism that had grown out of the bad relations between Catholics and Protestants in Europe. As a result, there were suspicions that Catholics could not be good citizens, that they owed allegiance to a foreign prince—the Pope. There was also suspicion that their church governments did not fit them out properly to be a democratic people. Popular sentiment held that as members of an authoritarian church, a church with a hierarchical structure, they could not really be good American citizens because they would not have formed the habits of mind necessary to be true citizens of a democratic republic. Of course, the Catholics were eventually able to prove that they were the best of good citizens. They died on the battlefield fighting for democracy in all the wars of American history. They proved their loyalty in so many other ways. And people eventually came to see that there was no contradiction, even of spirit, in belonging to a church with a hierarchical structure and also being citizens of a democracy in which all are equal in fundamental civil and political rights.

ROBERT GEORGE

Above: Methodist camp meeting.

Opposite Inset: The Dutch Church of Schenectady (1734–1814) in present-day Schenectady, New York.

Engraving, Prints and Photographs Division, Library of Congress. • Drawn for J. W. MacMurray, U.S.A., A. Wild Photo Engraving from the book, A History of the Schenectady Patent in the Dutch and English Times, J. W. MacMurray, ed., A. M., U. S. A. (Albany, NY: J. Munsell's Sons, Printers, 1883). • Courtesy of film First Freedom. Photographer, Mark Mabry.

thirteen disparate colonies. The Great Awakening also had the effect of eliding ethnic and language barriers as evangelicals of various backgrounds—Palatinate Lutherans, Dutch Reformed, Scottish Presbyterians, New England Congregationalists—cooperated in the venture of bringing enthusiastic religion to the masses. In central New Jersey, for instance, the Dutch Reformed minister Theodorus Jacobus Frelinghuysen and Gilbert Tennent, a Presbyterian, frequently preached in one another's pulpits, thereby toppling ethnic barriers that, a century earlier, would have kept them apart.

Taken together—Whitefield's use of persuasive oratory, the challenge of itinerants to the settled clergy, new patterns of communication, and falling ethnic barriers—the changes to American society wrought by the Great Awakening helped to set the stage for larger political changes later in the eighteenth century.

But no change that Whitefield and his fellow itinerants wrought was more significant than their populist appeal to the masses. Whitefield's skills as an orator were singular, but other evangelical preachers sought to mimic his style, many of them quite successfully. "The reading of Sermons is a dull way of Preaching," Solomon Stoddard, Jonathan Edwards's grandfather, had warned back in 1723. "Sermons when Read are not delivered with Authority and in an affecting way."[29]

The evangelical preachers of the Great Awakening took that warning to heart, and soon a chasm began to open between the staid preaching of the established, settled clergy and that of the energetic revival preachers. Samuel Davies, a Presbyterian, wrote to the bishop of London in 1752 to defend the dissenters of Hanover County, Virginia, and also to specify why so many people in Virginia were leaving Anglican churches for evangelical preachers. The reason, he said, was "the prospect of being entertained with more profitable doctrines among the dissenters than they were wont to hear in the parish churches." Davies, who would become president of the College of New Jersey (Princeton) in 1759, went on to explain the popular appeal of evangelicalism at the expense of the Anglican clergy who, in Davies's words, "generally entertain their hearers with languid harangues on morality or insipid speculations, omitting or but slightly touching upon the glorious doctrines of the gospel." Davies predicted that in any such contest, the evangelical preachers, with their popular appeal, would prevail.

The Great Awakening, like all movements built on religious fervor, waxed and then finally waned, but its greatest legacy was religious populism. No longer could clergy rely on their appointments as pastor of this or that church. In order to thrive—and sometimes simply to survive—they needed to appeal to the masses much the way Whitefield had. Without popular followings, these clergy would be bereft of their livings.

The Great Awakening, then, bequeathed an unmistakably populist flavor to American religion. Clergy competed with one another for popular followings, and to do so they adopted—as best they could—many of Whitefield's techniques, including persuasive oratory and extemporaneous preaching.

Even the venerable Jonathan Edwards, who was apparently not gifted at extemporaneous preaching, wrote his sermons in folios small enough to hide inside his palm so that he could convey the (mis)impression that he was not preaching from a prepared text.

By midcentury, when the Awakening had largely abated, the colonists were beginning to turn their attentions to matters other than religion; for all of the excitement associated with the revival, overall church attendance was little changed from what it had been prior to the Awakening. But the alterations in American society wrought by the revival—persuasive oratory, challenge to religious establishments, new patterns of communication, and, most of all, religious populism—were firmly ensconced in American life and would shape the formulation of the new nation.

The Great Awakening brought about a religious fervor among the colonists that saw women and freed slaves preaching to whomever would listen.

Courtesy of film First Freedom. *Photographer, Mark Mabry.*

3

The Road to
REVOLUTION

It is an indispensable duty, my brethren,

which we owe to God and our country,

to rouse up and bestir ourselves, and,

being animated with a noble zeal for

the sacred cause of liberty,

to defend our lives and fortunes,

even to the shedding of the last drop of blood.

— SAMUEL WEST —

"On the Right to Rebel Against Governors" (1776)[30]

By THE MIDDLE OF THE EIGHTEENTH CENTURY, RELIGIOUS LIFE IN THE COLONIES WAS JUST AS DIVERSE AS IT HAD BEEN A CENTURY EARLIER, PERHAPS MORE SO. The Great Awakening had leveled many ethnic barriers, but the spectrum of religious expression in America remained remarkably broad. Jews had settled in Atlantic seaports, from Newport to Charleston and Savannah. Roman Catholics were concentrated in Maryland, but they were also present on the fringes of colonial life in places like the Mohawk Valley of New York, Québec, and Florida. Folk religious practices flourished, both in backcountry areas as well alongside more "orthodox" expressions of faith in New England.

Among Protestants alone, the diversity was breathtaking. Baptists were flourishing. William Penn's hospitality toward religious dissenters lured various groups to his "Holy Experiment" in Pennsylvania, from the Moravians to the Schwenckfelders. Larger groups in the colonies included the Dutch Reformed Church,

Previous Page: Religious tolerance was still a new concept in colonial America. Baptist preacher Elijah Craig was imprisoned for not having a license from the Anglican Church in Virginia.

Right: Some colonists expressed their religious persecution by tarring and feathering those who had opposing views.

Courtesy of film First Freedom. *Photographer, Mark Mabry. • Courtesy Bridgeman Art Library, Boston Citizens Tar and Feather a Tax Collector. Color Litho; artist unknown.*

German Reformed, Lutherans, Presbyterians, and Anglicans (Church of England). The single largest group was the Congregationalists, the lineal descendants of the Puritans, but they accounted for only about 22 percent of the colonists.

This diversity presented the colonies with a quandary all but unique in the modern world: How to forge unity out of diversity.

In some places, authorities sought to coerce religious uniformity and conformity. In Virginia, for example, the Church of England was the established religion, and some magistrates were zealous in defense of Anglican prerogatives. Baptists, because of their insistence on religious liberty, often felt the sting of persecution. Baptists were thrown in jail in Spotsylvania in 1768 for disturbing the peace because of their preaching. A judge named Edmund Pendleton sentenced Baptist preachers to jail for what one contemporary called "the heinous charge of worshiping God according to the dictates of their own consciences." A sheriff brutally horsewhipped a Baptist minister, and a "gang of well-dressed men" nearly drowned two other Baptists by holding their heads underwater in a nearby river, a cynical riff on the Baptist insistence on believers' baptism by full immersion.[31]

Amid all this diversity and persecution, some colonists were beginning to warn publicly against the dangers of religious establishment. "It is not to be doubted," William Livingston—a graduate of Yale, activist in New York politics, and later the first governor of New Jersey—wrote in 1768 that "every man who wishes to be free will by all lawful ways in

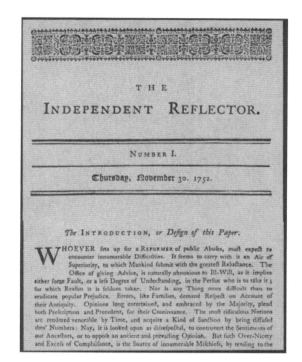

his power oppose the establishment of any one denomination in America." Remarking on "the inconveniences and mischiefs of religious establishments," Livingston concluded: "Religious establishments are very hardly kept from great corruption."[32]

Livingston had already proven his resistance to state support for religious institutions. As editor of the *Independent Reflector* in New York, Livingston had opposed the use of public funds for the formation of a college that would be run jointly by the Church of England with the collaboration of Dutch Reformed clergy. In 1746 the general assembly of New York had authorized a lottery to raise money for a college, but Livingston objected to the use of those proceeds to support a sectarian school. Livingston prevailed, and when King's College (now Columbia) was formed in 1754, it was built on land donated by Trinity Church, but it used no public funds.[33]

Despite this early victory for church-state separation, many of the colonies persisted in their practice of using taxpayer funds to support

In 1752, Livingston founded a weekly journal, *The Independent Reflector*. It was New York's first serial non-newspaper publication. *The Reflector* was used as a platform for challenging the De Lancey/Anglican faction, most notably over the founding of King's College. Publication of the journal ceased with the fifty-second issue after political pressure was brought to bear upon its printer, James Parker.

William Livingston (November 30, 1723 – July 25, 1790) attained considerable influence amongst the local patriots in New Jersey when he moved there from New York in 1770. Livingston was elected to serve as one of New Jersey's delegates to the Continental Congress and was a signer of the United States Constitution. In October 1775, he was commissioned a brigadier general of the New Jersey Militia. He then served as the governor of New Jersey (1776–1790).

Portrait by John Wollaston. Oil (undated). Sons of the Revolution, Fraunces Tavern Museum, New York City. Public domain because its copyright has expired. This applies to Australia, the European Union, and those countries with a copyright term of the author plus 70 years.

Below: Religious tolerance was still a new concept in Colonial America. Judge Edmund Pendleton, a delegate to the Constitutional Convention, sentenced Elijah Craig, a Baptist minister, to jail for teaching without a license from the dominant Virginian church, the Anglican Church.

Courtesy of film First Freedom. *Photographer, Mark Mabry.*

America's Strength in Religious Diversity

The religious diversity of the American colonists was obviously a point of division. But it was also important in unifying the country. The divisions were the result of differences of opinion. People took their religious faith seriously, as they do today, and although most were Protestants, there were a small number of Catholics who were involved in the American Revolution. Even the Protestants represented different forms of Protestantism—Baptists, Presbyterians, and Episcopalians—and they took their differences very seriously.

There were suspicions across the various religious divides. At the same time, the diversity of religious beliefs and opinions caused the colonists to look for a foundation for the American republic that would be solid enough that it wouldn't rest on the narrow doctrines of a particular Protestant faith, or even a particular Christian faith. They needed a set of principles that all could affirm in good conscience, be they Presbyterians, Baptists, Episcopalians, Catholics, or Jews. So when Thomas Jefferson and his committee that had been commissioned to write a Declaration of Independence came forward with their great work, colonists across the religious spectrum could affirm the words: "We hold these truths to be self-evident, that all men are created equal. That they are endowed by their creator with certain unalienable rights, and among these are life, liberty and the pursuit of happiness."

That core foundational belief did not rest on a specific religion. It was a generic, ethical, monotheistic belief that could be affirmed across the different lines of religious position but that still held great meaning. It expressed the proposition that our fundamental rights and dignity do not come as gifts from government, from a legislature, from a king, or from a president. Instead, they come from more than a merely human source—a divine source, God Himself. And since the government didn't confer those rights, the government has no legitimate power to take them away. Removing those rights would constitute violation of divine law. So the genius of the American founding was using religious diversity to come up with a founding principle that would transcend the divisions.

—————

ROBERT GEORGE

a particular denomination, thereby imposing a burden of both conscience and taxation on those who dissented from the established church. "We Have at our own Cost Settled a Minister & built a Meeting House for Divine Worship," a group of dissenters in Preston, Connecticut, wrote to their legislature in 1751. "Nevertheless we are Compelled to pay towards the Support of the Ministry & for the building of Meeting Houses In these Societies from which we have Respectively Sepperated and Desented." The dissenters pleaded for relief, asking to be "Released and Exempted from Paying Taxes for the Building of Meetinghouses or for the Support of the ministry in any of the Societies from which we have Sepperated."[34]

One person profoundly affected by the spectacle of religious coercion and persecution was a seventeen-year-old James Madison in Orange, Virginia. While walking with his father one day in 1768, the two men heard preaching coming from the local jail. Inside, Elijah Craig, a Baptist preacher, was orating from his cell. A crowd gathered, and young Madison took it all in. He didn't respond to the preacher's religious appeals, but he became a lifelong advocate of religious liberty. "That diabolical, hell-conceived principle of persecution rages," Madison wrote several years later. "There are, at present, in the adjacent county not less than five or six well-meaning men in close jail for publishing their religious sentiments," he continued. "I must beg you to pity me, and pray for liberty of conscience to all."[35]

Some dissenters detected in religious establishment the dreaded specter of Roman Catholicism. Yes, the ministers of the state churches wanted peace, Reuben Fletcher, who described himself as "an Independant," acknowledged, but "upon the same terms that the Pope is for peace, for he

Inset: Elijah Craig (1738/1743–May 18, 1808), a Baptist preacher arrested for teaching without a license in Virginia.

Below: Undeterred, Elijah Craig taught through the bars of his prison cell. Seventeen-year-old James Madison stopped and listened outside the jail cell, and was much affected by the persecution that had resulted in imprisonment for this man.

This is a faithful photographic reproduction of an original woodblock. The work of art itself is public domain because its copyright has expired. This applies to countries with a copyright term of life of the author plus 70 years. • Courtesy of film First Freedom. Photographer, Mark Mabry.

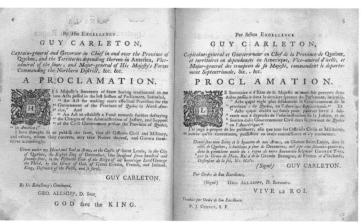

Top: Québec, Canada, in the eighteenth century.

Above Left: Sir Guy Carleton served as governor of the Province of Quebec from 1768 to 1778, concurrently serving as governor general of British North America during that time. While Carleton was in London, Parliament passed the Quebec Act of 1774 based on Carleton's recommendations.

Above Right: Excerpts from the Québec Act, passed by Parliament in 1774.

wants to rule over all Christians throughout the whole world, and they want to rule from one town to another, throughout the whole country." If the established clergy had their way, Fletcher continued, Baptists and other dissenters "would have no more liberties here than the protestants have in France or Rome."[36]

The aversion to Roman Catholicism harbored by most of the colonists exploded into something close to hysteria in the 1770s. Britain's victory in the French and Indian War in 1763 brought the territory of Lower Canada (Québec) under its control. In an effort to accommodate and to mollify the overwhelmingly French-speaking, Roman Catholic inhabitants, Parliament passed the Québec Act in 1774, which granted the people of Québec freedom to worship as they chose: "His Majesty's Subjects professing the Religion of the Church of Rome, of, and in the said Province of *Quebec,* may have, hold, and enjoy, the free Exercise of the Religion of the Church of Rome."

Colonists in America were furious, fearing that the ascendance of Catholicism anywhere in North America would threaten their own freedom of worship. The Québec Act, in the eyes of those who would become patriots, represented an utter betrayal of Protestantism. In Boston, Paul Revere drew a cartoon depicting Roman Catholic bishops dancing in celebration of the act. Samuel Adams joined the fray. "Much more is to be dreaded from the growth of POPERY in America," he declared, "than from Stamp-Acts or *any other* Acts destructive of men's *civil* rights."[37]

For many colonists, especially in New York and New England, the

Above: Paul Revere drew a cartoon mocking four mitred Anglican clergy for drawing up the Québec Act; a dark, winged Luciferian figure hovers behind them, whispering his counsel in their ears to encourage their "approbation and countenance of the Roman religion."

Right: Religious fervor had colonists gathering to listen to open air preachers.

Right: Seal of the Society for Propagating the Gospel in Foreign Parts. The Anglican Church was competing with Congregational churches in New England, and SPG missioners had to compete with numerous Baptist and Methodist preachers. The SPG helped promote better design for new churches, including the addition of steeples. The white church with steeple was copied by other groups and became associated with New England-style churches among the range of Protestant sects.

Below: When James Madison was just seventeen years old, he witnessed the jailing of Elijah Craig and was deeply affected by this religious persecution. A few years later, he would be credited with drafting the First Amendment to the Constitution, guaranteeing religious freedom in the new United States of America.

Courtesy of Anglicans Online • Courtesy of film First Freedom. Photographer, Mark Mabry.

specter of an Anglican bishop in the colonies was nearly as frightening as a Catholic one. Wearied of missionaries proselytizing for the Society for the Propagation of the Gospel and increasingly suspicious of Britain's imperialism, the colonists feared that the Church of England would dispatch a bishop to the colonies, thereby allowing for the ordination of Anglican priests in America and further extending Britain's authority over the colonies. Nathan Hobart of Stamford, Connecticut, argued in 1746 that any expansion of the Church of England would abet an "unnecessary and hurtful State of Dependence." Four years later, Jonathan Mayhew, a

Congregational minister in Boston, insisted that the sole defense against religious repression and thereby "being unmercifully priest-ridden" lay in "keeping all imperious bishops, and other clergymen who love to lord it over God's heritage, from getting their feet into the stirrup at all."[38]

At times, the fears over the prospect of an Anglican bishop grew to a fever pitch. Colonists believed that political and religious repression were substantially the same, that one abetted the other. The prospect of an Anglican bishop in the colonies "spread an universal alarm against the authority of Parliament," John Adams

wrote years later about the coming of the American Revolution. "It excited a general and just apprehension, that bishops, and dioceses, and churches, and priests, and tithes, were to be imposed on us by Parliament." Given the intimate connection between religious establishment and political coercion, Adams said, such apprehension was not without foundation: "If Parliament could tax us, they could establish the Church of England, with all its creeds, articles, tests, ceremonies, and tithes, and prohibit all other churches."[39]

With the approach of the American Revolution, the cast of players who would shape the configuration of church and state in the new nation was beginning to emerge. By any reckoning, it would be an odd and unlikely coalition, an improbable combination of Evangelicals like Isaac Backus, Unitarians like John Adams (Samuel Adams's cousin), and Deists like Benjamin Franklin and Thomas Jefferson.

Above Left: *Repression of the Church of England.* Showing the people below the clergy is symbolic of the repression of the church.

Above Right: John Adams (1735–1826).

Inset: An eloquent proponent of the idea that civil and religious liberty was ordained by God, Jonathan Mayhew considered the Church of England as a dangerous, almost diabolical enemy of the New England way. The bishop's mitre with the snake emerging from it represented his view of the Anglican hierarchy.

Courtesy Bridgeman Fine Art, Auto de Fe in the Plaza Mayor, Madrid, 30 June 1680, by Francisco Ricci. • John Adams, courtesy Pendleton's Lithography, circa 1828. • Etching by Giovanni Cipriani, London: 1767; The American Antiquarian Society, Worcester, Massachusetts. Library of Congress.

4

A PRAYER for a NATION to COME

I beg that I may not be understood to infer, that our General Convention was divinely inspired, when it form'd the new Constitution . . . yet I must own I have so much faith in the general Government of the world by Providence, that I can hardly conceive a Transaction of such momentous Importance to the Welfare of Millions now existing, and to exist in the Posterity of a great Nation, should be suffered to pass without being in some degree influenc'd, guided, and governed by that omnipotent, omnipresent, and beneficent Ruler, in whom all inferior Spirits live, move, and have their Being.

— BENJAMIN FRANKLIN —

"A Comparison of the Conduct of Ancient Jews and Anti-federalists in the United States of America" (1788)[40]

B Y THE AUTUMN OF 1774, BRITISH POLICIES LIKE THE STAMP ACT AND THE COERCIVE ACTS HAD INCENSED MANY AMERICANS AND BROUGHT THEM TO THE PRECIPICE OF REBELLION. Talk of revolution was in the air. Every colony except Georgia sent a delegation to Philadelphia to discuss what measures to take to resist what they saw as British imperialism. This first Continental Congress was the first time that the separate colonies had met in a single assembly.

As the crowds gathered outside, the delegates pondered how to open their deliberations. One of the delegates from Massachusetts proposed that they open in prayer. But what kind of prayer? The colonists themselves were divided; Congregationalists typically distrusted Anglicans and Quakers, and vice versa. As John Adams recalled, the motion to open with prayer "was opposed because we were so divided in religious sentiments—some were Episcopalians, some Quakers, some Anabaptists, some Presbyterians, and some Congregationalists—so that we could not join in the same act of worship." Samuel Adams, John Adams's cousin and a firebrand from Boston, rose and broke the deadlock. Pronouncing himself "no bigot," he allowed that he "could hear a prayer from any gentleman of piety and virtue, who was at the same time a friend to his country."[41]

A local Church of England priest was summoned, and, dressed in the ecclesiastical vestments that had so scandalized the Puritans a century earlier, he "read  the prayers in the established forms," according to John Adams, and then the thirty-fifth Psalm. "Plead my cause, O Lord, with them that strive with me," Jacob Duché, the priest, intoned. "Fight against them that fight against me." Having just received the news that the British had unleashed an attack in Boston the previous day, the delegates found those words especially comforting, "as if heaven had ordained that psalm to be read on that morning." After reading the Psalm, Duché launched into an extemporaneous prayer, which, according to Adams, "filled the bosom of every man present." The delegates took notice. "I must confess I never heard a better prayer," Adams, a Unitarian, wrote, "or one so well pronounced."[42]

With a religious crisis averted, the delegates turned their attention to matters at hand. The delegates drafted a letter to the Canadians, hoping to enlist their support in resisting the British. To do so, however, they had to persuade the Canadians that the freedom of religion granted by the Québec Act was not an extraordinary concession, that the freedom of religious expression was an inherent right. "And what is offered to you by the late act of parliament in their place?" the congress asked. "Liberty of conscience in your religion? No. God gave it to you."[43]

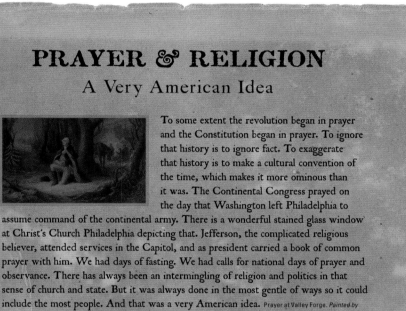

PRAYER & RELIGION
A Very American Idea

To some extent the revolution began in prayer and the Constitution began in prayer. To ignore that history is to ignore fact. To exaggerate that history is to make a cultural convention of the time, which makes it more ominous than it was. The Continental Congress prayed on the day that Washington left Philadelphia to assume command of the continental army. There is a wonderful stained glass window at Christ's Church Philadelphia depicting that. Jefferson, the complicated religious believer, attended services in the Capitol, and as president carried a book of common prayer with him. We had days of fasting. We had calls for national days of prayer and observance. There has always been an intermingling of religion and politics in that sense of church and state. But it was always done in the most gentle of ways so it could include the most people. And that was a very American idea. *Prayer at Valley Forge. Painted by Henry Brueckner. Engraved by John O. McRae. Published by Joseph Lang, London, Edinburgh, New York.*

—///////—

JON BUTLER

As the colonists headed toward revolution, the Continental Congress persuaded a reluctant Virginian, George Washington, to command the Continental Army. Washington, a Mason who was not conventionally religious, nevertheless understood the importance of religious toleration. "I trust the people of every denomination will be convinced that I shall always strive to prove a faithful and impartial patron of genuine, vital religion," Washington wrote to the Methodist bishops in 1789. "No one would be more zealous than myself to establish effectual barriers against the horrors of spiritual tyranny and every species of religious persecution."[44]

Washington sought to live by those ideals. When he commissioned Benedict Arnold to undertake a military campaign to persuade the people of Québec to cooperate in resisting the British, Washington instructed Arnold to show religious toleration. "Contempt of the Religion of a Country by ridiculing any of its Ceremonies or affronting its Ministers or Votaries has ever been deeply resented," he wrote. "You are to be particularly careful to restrain every Officer and Soldier from such Imprudence and Folly and to punish every Instance of it." Having warned against intolerance, the general continued: "On the other hand, as far as lays in your power, you are to protect and support the free Exercise of the Religion of the Country and the undisturbed Enjoyment of Conscience in religious Matters, with your utmost Influence and Authority."[45]

Arnold's military campaign to Québec failed in its mission to enlist the Canadians in the struggle against Britain. Canada would remain British, but Washington nevertheless had established the point that the cause of American liberty would include freedom of religion.

For the Patriots, however, justifying rebellion against the monarch was dicey. For centuries, kings were thought to enjoy a "divine right" to rule over their subjects, so rebellion against the crown was not to be undertaken lightly. The colonists turned to John

Locke, the seventeenth-century English philosopher who, in his *Two Treatises on Government*, argued that everyone possessed a natural right to defend "life, health, liberty, or possessions." Each individual possessed natural rights, Locke argued, whereas any right granted by the king could also be rescinded by the king.

In the summer of 1776, a committee of five—including Thomas Jefferson, John Adams, and Benjamin Franklin—set to work drafting a document of rebellion against the king of England. The Declaration of Independence mentioned God four times, twice in the opening two sentences, but it relied heavily on Locke's notion of natural rights. "The Laws of Nature and Nature's God," the Declaration said, entitled the American people to be both equal to the British

George Washington confers with an aide at Valley Forge headquarters, Valley Forge, Pennsylvania.

"George Washington is an interesting religious figure. On the one hand, he can be seen as someone who soft-pedaled religious issues. On the other hand, Washington was a dutiful member of the Church of England, a reasonably regular attender of religious services, mostly at his own parish in the Church of England. He was someone who appreciated the link between religion, morals, and ethics, and he thought that difference was important. Washington was not overly pious. If you read Washington's diaries or any of his letters, you won't find a lot in them about religion. He wasn't someone who discussed his religion frequently but he clearly was a religious individual. He was a model for many American presidents who have seen their own religion as something personal but not necessarily something to be marketed to the nation as a whole." —Jon Butler

Inset Right: John Locke

Inset Left: Benedict Arnold

In 1776, the Declaration of Independence was drafted by a committee of five: John Adams of Massachusetts, Roger Sherman of Connecticut, Robert Livingston of New York, Benjamin Franklin of Pennsylvania, and Thomas Jefferson of Virginia.

Courtesy of film First Freedom. *Photographer, Mark Mabry.* • Committee of Congress Drafting the Declaration of Independence, *engraving by T. D. Booth.*

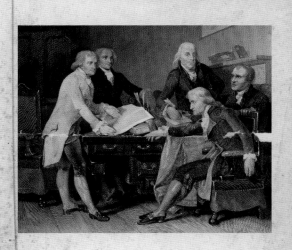

Religiouſ Forceſ in the Declaration & the Conſtitution

The foundational documents of the American experiment, the Declaration of Independence and the Constitution, can't be read in isolation one from another. The Declaration is founded on the idea that there is a Creator, a God who has created the world and endowed all of us with certain inalienable rights. Therefore, those rights are sacred. They cannot be tampered with by either the mob or the king. On the other hand, except for prohibiting a religious task for

federal office, the only other reference to religion in the original Constitution is a utilitarian one: "The year of our Lord 1787." I think you need both because, in fact, we don't have a godless Constitution.

I also don't think it is impossible to be a Christian nation. We were a nation that was attempting to find ways to respect the rights of believers to pursue their religious lives in as free a context as possible, knowing that those religious values would be brought to the public arena—just as any personal value is going to find expression in the government and in politics. But the Constitution determined how to manage that process—and I don't think there has ever been a better achievement anywhere in the world of both affirming and asserting. The Declaration asserts and affirms that religion is a force in the lives of men—that we are created, that we are endowed by that Creator with certain rights, and that nobody can tamper with them. The Constitution asserts and affirms that we are going to be rational and even-handed about the role of religion in society—in the same way we are rational and even-handed about the role of economics or geography or partisanship in our society. Taken together, they are the two wings on which we rose to the heights we now occupy.

—⁓—

JON MEACHAM

and separate from them. And all men "are endowed by their Creator with certain inalienable Rights," including "Life, Liberty and the Pursuit of Happiness." The third reference to God was an appeal to "the Supreme Judge of the world"; the fourth acknowledged "the protection of divine Providence."

The Declaration of Independence did not mention Christianity specifically, nor did it invoke orthodox Christian constructs like the deity of Jesus or the doctrine of the Trinity, which would have been objectionable to Unitarians like John Adams. The founders understood that, given the religious diversity already present in the American colonies, it was essential to craft a religiously generic document. But all could agree on the basic equality of all human beings who were, in the words of the Declaration, "endowed by their creator with certain inalienable rights."

But, tragically, not all human beings enjoyed those rights. "The Sin of Slavery," Abigail Adams wrote to her husband, John, "is not washed away." Dozens of the founders owned slaves, including Washington, Franklin, and Jefferson, the man who had penned the immortal words that "all men are created equal." Jefferson professed his abhorrence of the institution of slavery and of any slaveholder who would "inflict on his fellow men a bondage, one hour of which is fraught with more misery than ages of that which he rose in rebellion to oppose." Yet in his refusal to release his own slaves from bondage, Jefferson was describing himself.

Jefferson and the other founders justified their refusal to renounce slavery by appealing to pragmatism; they needed the support of the Southern colonies, including slaveholders,

Opposite: Thomas Jefferson held many slaves at Monticello, as did George Washington at his estate at Mt. Vernon.

Below: Slaves were used for a number of things, among them picking cotton on the plantations of the South.

Courtesy of film First Freedom. *Photographer, Mark Mabry.* • Slaves Pick Cotton on a Georgia Plantation, *wood engraving from Ballou's Pictorial Drawing Room Companion, January 23, 1858, by M. M. Ballou. Courtesty Prints and Photographs Division, Library of Congress.*

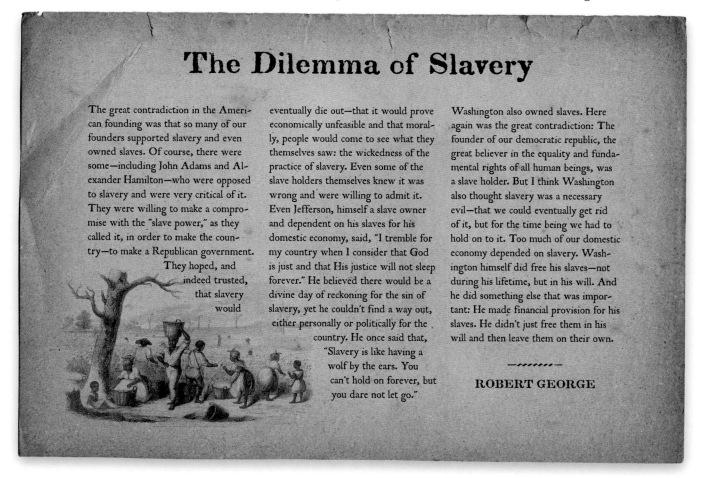

The Dilemma of Slavery

The great contradiction in the American founding was that so many of our founders supported slavery and even owned slaves. Of course, there were some—including John Adams and Alexander Hamilton—who were opposed to slavery and were very critical of it. They were willing to make a compromise with the "slave power," as they called it, in order to make the country—to make a Republican government. They hoped, and indeed trusted, that slavery would

eventually die out—that it would prove economically unfeasible and that morally, people would come to see what they themselves saw: the wickedness of the practice of slavery. Even some of the slave holders themselves knew it was wrong and were willing to admit it. Even Jefferson, himself a slave owner and dependent on his slaves for his domestic economy, said, "I tremble for my country when I consider that God is just and that His justice will not sleep forever." He believed there would be a divine day of reckoning for the sin of slavery, yet he couldn't find a way out, either personally or politically for the country. He once said that, "Slavery is like having a wolf by the ears. You can't hold on forever, but you dare not let go."

Washington also owned slaves. Here again was the great contradiction: The founder of our democratic republic, the great believer in the equality and fundamental rights of all human beings, was a slave holder. But I think Washington also thought slavery was a necessary evil—that we could eventually get rid of it, but for the time being we had to hold on to it. Too much of our domestic economy depended on slavery. Washington himself did free his slaves—not during his lifetime, but in his will. And he did something else that was important: He made financial provision for his slaves. He didn't just free them in his will and then leave them on their own.

—

ROBERT GEORGE

THE PARTING "Buy us too."

Though John Adams shuddered when considering the "calamities" that slavery was "likely to produce," many of the founders—including George Washington and Thomas Jefferson—had slaves at their estates in the colonies.

The Parting: "Buy Us Too." Artist, Henry Louis Stephens, circa 1863; courtesy of the Library of Congress. • Courtesy of film First Freedom. *Photographer, Mark Mabry.*

to maintain the unity of the colonies against Britain. At the same time, Jefferson recognized that the issue would erupt, later if not sooner. "I tremble for my country when I reflect that God is just," Jefferson wrote in 1781, "that his justice cannot sleep forever." John Adams, Jefferson's fellow founder, echoed those sentiments: "I shudder when I think of the calamities which slavery is likely to produce in this country."[46]

Thomas Jefferson and John Adams would become political adversaries, and later, after their presidencies, rekindle their friendship. Both of them died on the same day—July 4, 1826, fifty years to the day after the signing of the Declaration of Independence. They missed by a couple of decades their nation's final conflagration over slavery.

John Adams and his wife, Abigail, faithfully wrote letters to each other throughout the entire period during which the Continental Congress met; the letters have helped historians understand a significant chapter of American colonial history.

Courtesy of film First Freedom. Photographer, Mark Mabry.

CHAPTER

5

The Intent of
PROVIDENCE

*But I must submit
all my Hopes and Fears,
to an overruling Providence,
in which, unfashionable as
the Faith may be,
I firmly believe.*

— JOHN ADAMS —

Letter to Abigail Adams (1776)

Previous Page: In 1775, the Revolutionary War officially began. George Washington, appointed by the Continental Congress in April, led the Continental Army, hardly a match for the British army and navy. A few of Washington's soldiers wore mismatched uniforms, though many did not.

Above: John André, the spy who worked with Benedict Arnold in an attempt to turn over the vital West Point stronghold.

Right: Under General Washington, the Continental Army first occupied West Point on the Hudson River in 1778.

B Y MAY 1778, FOLLOWING THE BRUTAL WINTER AT VALLEY FORGE, MANY OF THE COLONISTS WERE DISPIRITED. The British army appeared to have the upper hand, while the Continental soldiers were poorly paid, badly fed, and sometimes overwhelmed by their odds against the Redcoats. What could possibly hold the ragtag army together, much less the colonists themselves, divided as they were by region, ethnicity, and religion?

The task of forging some measure of unity out of diversity fell on George Washington, commander of the Continental Army. Although he had been baptized as an Anglican, Washington was never confirmed, and he rarely took Holy Communion. He occasionally declared days of thanksgiving to mark a military victory, but even then he had to tread carefully. The Sabbath (Sunday) was observed as a day of rest in New England and a day of recreation in Virginia. Such days of thanksgiving, Washington decided, would be marked by rest in the morning and recreation in the afternoon.

Despite his own tepid religious views, Washington recognized the importance of faith, both for himself and others. "No Man has a more perfect Reliance on the alwise, and powerful dispensations of the Supreme Being than I have nor thinks his aid more necessary," he wrote to William Gordon in 1776. Washington authorized the appointment of chaplains to the army, believing that faith inculcates virtue. Appealing to Congress for better pay for the chaplains, Washington wrote: "I need not point out the great utility of Gentlemen whose lives and conversations are unexceptionable, being employed for that service in this Army."[47]

For Washington and many other founders, direct references to God did not come easily; they preferred to talk about divine providence. And for Washington, nothing demonstrated the workings of divine providence more dramatically than the West Point affair, a fortuitous event that once again involved Benedict Arnold. In 1779, Washington gave Benedict Arnold command of the vital West Point stronghold on the Hudson River north of New York City. Arnold,

Above: General Washington had chaplains appointed to the Continental Army to encourage religious worship, regardless of an individual's faith.

Left: John André was detained and arrested as a spy for trying to turn the West Point garrison over to the British.

Courtesy of film First Freedom. *Photographer, Mark Mabry.*

however, was a traitor; he devised a plot to turn West Point over to the British and gave the papers detailing his plan to a spy named John André, who disguised himself in an American uniform and rushed with the plans toward British headquarters in New York.

The next morning a wandering group of American soldiers, absent without leave from the Continental Army, stopped André for no reason at all. They searched him and discovered the papers, thereby foiling Arnold's treasonous plot. "In no instance, since the commencement of the war," Washington recounted, "has the interposition of Providence appeared more remarkably conspicuous than in the rescue of the post and garrison of West Point from Arnold's villainous perfidy."[48]

The invoking, and the crediting, of providence allowed the founding generation to speak with some unity on matters of religion, without being overly specific about whose God—or whose providence—they meant. Among a religiously diverse people, references to "providence" could be generic, without favoring or offending any religious group. But the invocations of providence also provided assurance that some larger entity was looking after the interests of the colonists, and incidents like the Benedict Arnold affair at West Point and crucial military victories provided much-needed affirmation. Just as John Winthrop believed that Massachusetts would be the "city on a hill," now the colonists began to think that their fledgling nation enjoyed the benefits of divine providence.

Right: Sermons, like this one from clergy Abraham Keteltas, supported colonial revolutionary ideas by saying that God and biblical authority backed their quest for freedom.

Below: General George Washington at camp tent headquarters.

"Religion and the Founding of the American Republic" sermon; courtesy, Library of Congress. • Courtesy of film First Freedom. Photographer, Mark Mabry.

Left: James Caldwell (1734–1781), a Presbyterian minister at Elizabeth, New Jersey, was one of the many clergymen who served as chaplains during the Revolutionary War. At the battle of Springfield, New Jersey, on June 23, 1780, when his company ran out of wadding, Caldwell was said to have dashed into a nearby Presbyterian church, scooped up as many Watts hymnals as he could carry, and distributed them to the troops, shouting "put Watts into them, boys." Caldwell and his wife were both killed before the war ended.

Above: Peter Muhlenberg (1746–1807) was the prime example of a "fighting parson" during the Revolutionary War. The eldest son of Lutheran patriarch Henry Melchoir Muhlenberg, young Muhlenberg at the conclusion of a sermon in January 1776 to his congregation in Woodstock, Virginia, threw off his clerical robes to reveal the uniform of a Virginia militia officer. Having served with distinction throughout the war, Muhlenberg commanded a brigade that successfully stormed the British lines at Yorktown. He retired from the Army in 1783 as a brevetted major general.

Both images on this page courtesy Library of Congress, "Religion and the Founding of the American Republic" Exhibition. Reverend James Caldwell at the Battle of Springfield. Watercolor by Henry Alexander Ogden. Presbyterian Historical Society, Philadelphia. • John Peter Gabriel Muhlenberg. Oil on canvas, by an unidentified nineteenth-century American artist. Martin Art Gallery, Muhlenberg College, Allentown, Pennsylvania.

Other colonists had no qualms whatsoever about invoking the Almighty in the patriots' struggle against Britain. Preaching at the Presbyterian church in Newburyport, Massachusetts, on October 5, 1777, Abraham Keteltas characterized the Revolution as "the cause of truth, against error and falsehood" and "the cause of pure and undefiled religion, against bigotry, superstition, and human invention." Other clergy, like James Caldwell, a Presbyterian from New Jersey, and Peter Muhlenberg, a Lutheran from Virginia, joined the military struggle, either as chaplains, or combatants, or both.

Even as the military conflict raged between British forces and the Continental Army, some of the founders began to consider the outlines of a new government, and not least among their deliberations was the relationship between church and state. Ever since its founding, the government of Virginia had been closely intertwined with the Church of England, but as the war continued the political leaders in Virginia began to consider a different configuration.

Virginia, like many of the other colonies, was venturing into new territory. Although some of the colonies—Rhode Island, New York, and Pennsylvania, among others—effectively had no state church, others—like Massachusetts, Connecticut, and Virginia—clung to their religious establishments, even if they made the designation more generic. The constitution of South Carolina, for example, stipulated that the "Christian Protestant Religion shall be deemed, and is hereby constituted and declared to be the established religion of this State."[49]

Some of the political leaders in Virginia, however, began to consider alternatives. The initial draft of the Virginia Declaration of Rights, written

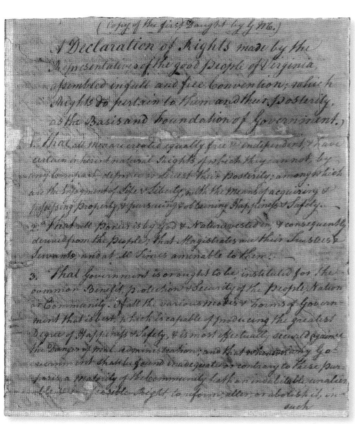

The Virginia Declaration of Rights (bottom), authored by George Mason (top), was a precursor to the wording and intent of the Declaration of Independence, authored by Thomas Jefferon, and later served as a model for the first ten amendments to the Constitution, also known as the Bill of Rights.

Etched by Albert Rosenthal, 1888. • Manuscript. George Mason Papers, Manuscript Division, Library of Congress.

by George Mason, included a clause that guaranteed toleration of all religious expression: "All men should enjoy the fullest toleration in the exercise of religion, according to the dictates of conscience, unpublished and unrestrained by the magistrate." James Madison, however, who had been so scandalized by the government's treatment of Baptists, thought that Mason's proposal did not go far enough. The notion of toleration, in fact, struck Madison as condescending, even paternalistic, because it implied that the entity granting toleration—whether religion, government, or an individual—had the authority to grant toleration. Madison disagreed, recognizing that if toleration can be granted, it could also be withdrawn. This violated Locke's notion of natural rights, that rights were inherent and not bestowed by any human entity.[50]

Even some ministers, Baptists in particular, agreed. "Government should protect every man in thinking and speaking freely, and see that one does not abuse another," wrote John Leland, a Baptist preacher who had befriended Thomas Jefferson during his time in Virginia. "The liberty I contend for is more than toleration. The very idea of toleration is despicable; it supposes that some have a pre-eminence above the rest to grant indulgence, whereas all should be equally free, Jews, Turks, Pagans and Christians."[51]

Madison quietly set about rewriting Mason's draft. The final version of the Virginia Declaration of Rights, adopted in 1776, asserted "that religion, or the duty which we owe to our Creator, and the manner of discharging it, can be directed only by reason and conviction, not by force or violence;

The WALL of SEPARATION BETWEEN CHURCH and STATE

Richard Hooker. State 1. By Wenzel Hollar (1607–1677), University of Toronto Wenceslaus Hollar Digital Collection.

The phrase *the wall of separation between church and state* comes from the Anglican Divine Richard Hooker. It was originally intended to signify that the church needed protection from the state. As Roger Williams said, "The wilderness of the world is dangerous for the Garden of Christ's Church." It is a low wall, it seems to me. It is a hedge—it is, as a friend of mine once said, a chain-link fence. And there is a lot to that. You can't separate religion and politics. But you can, and you should, separate church and state. And it is that distinction that will lower everyone's blood pressure as they debate various issues that come up in the first years of the twenty-first century. Religious expression, religious conversation in the public square, is part of the American fabric because it is part of what people value—and what is a republic but an expression of what people value? But we should not make decisions entirely on religious grounds, any more than we should make decisions entirely on economic grounds or entirely on geographic grounds or entirely on partisan grounds. And what the Madisonian construct gives us is the ability to have all of these voices in the arena fighting it out, checks and balances, the ability to curb excesses, and the chance to see what wins and who wins. And the brilliance of the republic is that we can have these fights—but we are shouting and talking, not shooting.

— ✦ —

JON MEACHAM

The separation of church and state worked in the new nation because the new nation was a pluralistic community of many different religions. There was no way that one group was going to be able to establish itself as the official church, and the framers knew that. They themselves represented many different denominations, and they had bitter experience in some places with establishments that had been rejected. The states still continued some requirements of being a Christian or a Trinitarian in order to hold office at the state level. But at the federal level there was no question that that was possible. On the other hand, they did believe that religion was a support for moral and social order and that it was important—and they believed that it should be allowed to be practiced freely. All of the founders—including Jefferson and Madison and Franklin and Washington and others—understood that well. Free religion, un-coerced, was to be the American way.

— ✦ —

PATRICIA BONOMI

The First Amendment and the Bill of Rights

Those who designed the Constitution didn't originally envision a "bill of rights," but they quickly realized that they needed to reassure colonists about the limits and character of this new federal government. And so they designed a series of amendments. It isn't entirely clear that the First Amendment was meant to be the first amendment; it just happened to be the first and it just happened to deal with two critical issues: the freedom of speech and the freedom of religion.

Why were they interested in religion? Because religion had provoked so many problems, both in Europe and in a number of the American colonies, that they greatly feared the ability of the federal government to potentially establish a single state church in a society in which there were already many religions.

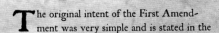

Religious Freedom IN AMERICA
1657
THE FLUSHING REMONSTRANCE
1957
3¢ UNITED STATES POSTAGE

3¢ U.S Postage Stamp, issued in 1957, celebrating 300 years of American religious freedom. Public domain in the United States—work prepared by an officer or employee of the United States Government as part of that person's official duties under the terms of Title 17, Chapter 1, Section 105 of the US Code.

There was great fear that the federal government might be able to establish a single church that would create enormous controversy over religion throughout the nation. And so the First Amendment both prohibited the establishment of any kind of religion sponsored by the federal government and protected the right to freedom of worship of any religion. The founders understood very well that they weren't giving a limited right to just a few religions for worship—they were giving the right for the practice of all religions—everything from Christianity to Islam and everything in between.

▩ ▩ ▩

The original intent of the First Amendment was very simple and is stated in the First Amendment itself: *Congress shall make no law respecting an establishment of religion.* In other words, those who drafted the document didn't want the federal government to be shaping American religion. They believed religion could shape itself. And the state of this nation at the beginning of the twenty-first century suggests that they could not have been more correct. We now live in a society that has far more religions, far more religious participation, and far more religion involved in society than we did at the time of the American Revolution and the creation of the first amendment. That fact alone is testament to the conviction that religion would flourish on its own. Religion would always flourish best when it wasn't associated with government. And the history of the United States over the past more than two hundred years suggests that this was one of the truly prophetic utterances of those who established our government.

— ✦ —

JON BUTLER

Above: Maps of the American colonies and of France.

Right: James Madison.

Inset, Below Right: John Jay was the first chief justice of the United States (1789–1795) and served as the president of the Continental Congress from 1778 to 1779. During and after the American Revolution, Jay was a minister (ambassador) to Spain and France, helping to fashion United States foreign policy. His major diplomatic achievement was to negotiate favorable trade terms with Great Britain in the Jay Treaty of 1794. A proponent of strong, centralized government, Jay worked to ratify the new Constitution in New York in 1788 by anonymously writing a few of the Federalist Papers along with the main authors, Alexander Hamilton and James Madison.

Maps created by Adam Hill. • James Madison. Etching made from the original series painted by Stuart. • John Jay. Portrait by Gilbert Stuart (1755–1828), National Gallery of Art. Public domain in the United States and those countries with a copyright term of life of the author plus 100 years or less.

and therefore all men are equally entitled to the free exercise of religion, according to the dictates of conscience; and that it is the mutual duty of all to practice Christian forbearance, love, and charity toward each other." Freedom, Madison insisted, was superior to toleration, a principle that the founders would eventually enshrine in the First Amendment. "I will not condescend to employ the word Toleration," John Adams reflected many years later. "I assert that unlimited freedom of religion, consistent with morals and property, is essential to the progress of society and the amelioration of the condition of mankind."[52]

Madison's emendations represented a step forward for religious liberty, but the clause had also specified the centrality of Christianity to any scheme of social order: "It is the mutual duty of all to practice Christian forbearance, love, and charity toward each other." On this point, Jefferson entered the discussion. He drafted an Act for Establishing Religious Freedom, which expanded even further the right to affiliate with any religion or with none at all. Jefferson took copies of his proposed legislation with him when he was appointed minister to France. The thinkers of Europe, after all, had laid the groundwork for

the great experiment in freedom and natural rights that was unfolding on the western shores of the Atlantic. Europeans may have produced the ideas, but Americans were setting them in motion.

Despite his efforts, however, Jefferson's bill stalled in the legislature.

Following the defeat of Charles Cornwallis and the British forces at Yorktown, John Adams, Benjamin Franklin, and John Jay

Bill of Rights

Article 1 reads: Congress shall make no law respecting an establishment of religion, or prohibiting the free exercise thereof; or abridging the freedom of speech, or of the press; or the right of the people peaceably to assemble, and to petition the Government for a redress of grievances.

Above: Naval battle of the *Bon Homme Richard* captained by John Paul Jones.

Right: The Battle of Lexington and Concord, where the first shot fired against the British in the American Revolution occurred; the battle was fought by men who were mostly not professional soldiers.

The Memorable Engagement Of Capt. N Pearson Of *The Serapis*, With Paul Jones Of *The Bon Homme Richard* & His Squadron, Sep. 23 1779. *Painting by Richard Patton; engravers, Daniel Lerpinière and James Fittler; courtesy the Robert Charles Lawrence Fergusson Collection, The Society of the Cincinnati.* • *The Battle of Lexington. Engraving by John H. Daniels & Son, Library of Congress.*

Above: Battle of Bunker Hill

Battle of Bunker Hill, *E. Percy Moran, Library of Congress.*

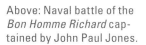

Why America Won the Revolutionary War

America was not the center of the world. England was the center of the world, and so I think Britain was slow to understand the nature of the threat. I think we were a hearty bunch devoted to an idea that was not an abstract idea. It was quite real. It was the idea of personal liberty and self-government for white men, but we ultimately did better at expanding the promise. People fighting for Britain were fighting for the idea of an empire or were being paid to do it. People who were fighting for America, with the exception of some mercenaries we had to hire from Germany, were fighting for something more personal—and you always fight better, you always fight more strongly, you always fight more devotedly for something that is personal. This was about how you were going to run your life and whether your family was going to prosper. It wasn't about king and country.

—///——

JON MEACHAM

Minuteman. *Edward Eggleston, A First Book in American History (New York: American Book Company, 1889), 117.*

gathered at the Hotel d'York on September 3, 1783, to affix their signatures to the Treaty of Paris. David Hartley, a member of Parliament, signed on behalf of George III, king of Great Britain. The treaty marked the improbable victory of the Continental Army over the Redcoats and acknowledged the United States as an independent, sovereign nation with territory that stretched from the Atlantic Ocean to the Mississippi River and from Florida to the Great Lakes.

The patriots had been vindicated in their struggle against a superior military power. Surely, in the eyes of many, they had enjoyed divine favor. "I was but the humble agent of favoring heaven," George Washington wrote, "whose benign interference was so often manifested in our behalf, and to whom the praise of victory alone is due."[53]

With military victory behind them and independence assured, the founders now faced the daunting task of

Above: Lord Cornwallis surrendered Yorktown to George Washington on October 19, 1781. The terms of surrender were documented in a formal "Articles of Capitulation."

Inset: The Revolutionary War officially ended with the signing of the Treaty of Paris on Sept. 3, 1783.

Both images taken from: E. Benjamin Andrews, History of the United States from the Earliest Discovery of American to the Present Day (New York: Charles Scribner's Sons, 1895), 2:136–137. Florida Center for Instructional Technology, College of Education, University of South Florida.

Top: George Washington, 1732–1799, became trained as a military officer for the British in the French and Indian War.

Bottom: At Fraunces Tavern on December 4, 1783, Washington formally bade his officers farewell. On December 23, 1783, he resigned his commission as commander-in-chief, emulating the Roman general Cincinnatus, an exemplar of the republican ideal of citizen leadership who rejected power. During this period, the United States was governed without a president under the Articles of Confederation, the forerunner to the Constitution.

Courtesy of film First Freedom. *Photographer, Mark Mabry.* • George Washington Resigning His Commission *by John Trumbull, circa 1817, Architect of the Capitol.*

setting up a new political order, one that would embody the principles that had animated their rebellion against the British. Many of the colonies persisted in their taxation of citizens to support an established church. Jefferson disagreed, arguing that "to compel a man to furnish contributions of money for the propagation of opinions which he disbelieves and abhors, is sinful and tyrannical." Furthermore, Jefferson continued, "even the forcing him to support this or that teacher of his own religious persuasion, is depriving him of the comfort of giving his contributions to the particular pastor whose morals he would make his pattern, and whose powers he feels most persuasive to righteousness."[54]

Jefferson's ideas by no means enjoyed universal approbation. In Virginia, Patrick Henry had been persuaded by arguments against supporting any one religious denomination, even his own Church of England, the established church of the colony of Virginia. As an attorney, he had defended both Quakers and Baptists; in one memorable summation, he thundered that "Heaven decreed that man should be free—free to worship God according to the Bible." But Henry also believed that religion was an essential component of morality, and therefore the government should provide support for Christianity.

On the face of it, Henry's proposed Bill Establishing A Provision for Teachers of the Christian Religion represented a logical compromise between an established church and no public support whatsoever for any particular religion. He argued that the "general diffusion of Christian knowledge hath a natural tendency to correct

the morals of men, restrain their vices, and preserve the peace of society." He also asserted that his tax for the support of Christianity could be enacted "without counteracting the liberal principle heretofore adopted and intended to be preserved by abolishing all distinctions of pre-eminence amongst the different societies or communities of Christians."[55]

Patrick Henry, a fiery orator best known for his "give me liberty or give me death" speech, was a popular figure in Virginia,

Inset, Left: Patrick Henry (May 29, 1736–June 6, 1799), a fiery orator from Virginia, was a prominent figure in the American Revolution.

Below: At the conclusion of the Revolutionary War, George Washington retired to his home at Mt. Vernon, Virginia.

Benson Lossing, Harper's Encyclopedia of United States History (New York: Harper & Brothers Publishers, 1912), 4; Henry, Patrick. Florida Center for Instructional Technology, College of Education, University of South Florida. • Courtesy of film First Freedom. Photographer, Mark Mabry.

having been elected governor four times. Madison and Jefferson, both of whom opposed Henry's designation of Christianity as the state religion, faced an uphill political battle. Fearing that the assembly would quickly pass the bill, they prevailed on the legislators to postpone action to allow the proposal to circulate among the people of Virginia.

Patrick Henry and George Mason, representing their Baptist constituency, strongly urged James Madison to draft a series of amendments to the newly ratified U. S. Constitution. Unwilling at first, Madison later drafted the first amendments to the Bill of Rights.

Courtesy of film First Freedom. *Photographer, Mark Mabry.*

Popular reactions were mixed. "The Episcopal people are generally for it," Madison reported to James Monroe in April 1785. "The laity of the other sects are generally unanimous on the other side." That alignment might have been predicted, but Madison was especially miffed at the Presbyterian clergy, who had opposed the Anglican establishment in years past but were now "ready to set up an establishment" from which they would benefit. The general committee of Baptists, on the other hand, true to their tradition of religious liberty and wary of state interference in matters of faith, resolved "to oppose the law for a general assessment." A subsequent gathering of this group, meeting in Powhatan, reiterated Baptist opposition, arguing that it was "repugnant to the spirit of the gospel for the Legislature thus to proceed in matters of religion." The resolution affirmed that "every person ought to be left entirely free in respect to matters of religion."[56]

As handbills containing the text of Henry's proposed legislation circulated throughout Virginia, democracy took its course. "The printed bill

has excited great discussion," Madison reported. Only a month after his earlier letter to Monroe, Madison detected a change in popular sentiments. "The adversaries to the assessment begin to think the prospect here flattering to their wishes," he wrote. Even the Presbyterian clergy were reconsidering their earlier support, "either compelled by the laity of that sect or alarmed at the probability of farther interference of the Legislature, if they begin to dictate in matters of religion."[57]

Madison himself was hardly silent on the matter. He drafted an argument against Henry's bill, his *Memorial and Remonstrance Against Religious Assessments*, which would become a classic statement of opposition to religious establishment and a defense of religious liberty. "Who does not see that the same authority by which we can establish Christianity, in exclusion of all other religions, may establish with the same ease any particular sect of Christians, in exclusion of all other sects?" Madison asked. The majoritarianism implicit in Henry's argument that Christianity should receive state support because it was the faith of a majority of Virginians,

Left: As a lawyer and a fierce defender of freedom and equality, Patrick Henry defended Baptist clergy at no charge.

Below: Patrick Henry in the Virginia Assembly, where he gave his famous speech that included the oft-quoted phrase, "Give me liberty or give me death."

Courtesy of film First Freedom. Photographer, Mark Mabry. • Patrick Henry before the Virginia House of Burgesses, May 30, 1765, Alfred Jones; engraver, Peter Frederick Rothermel, 1852. Library of Congress.

Madison argued, was perilous because of the fact that "the majority may trespass on the rights of the minority." Madison's *Memorial* linked religious establishments with the sort of tyranny that the colonists had only recently resisted. "Torrents of blood have been spilt in the old world, by vain attempts of the secular arm to extinguish religious discord, by proscribing all difference in religious opinions," he wrote. Historically, religious establishments "have been seen upholding the thrones of political tyranny," he argued. "In no instance have they been seen the guardians of the liberties of the people." Religion, Madison wrote, "must be left to the conviction and conscience of every man; and it is the right over every man to exercise it as these may dictate."[58]

In addition to Madison's *Memorial and Remonstrance*, Virginians themselves weighed in on Patrick Henry's proposal;

Thomas Jefferson considered the passage of the Virginia Statute for Religious Freedom among his most significant achievements.

Opposite: Thomas Jefferson at his estate, Monticello, near Charlottesville, Virginia.

Document courtesy Library of Congress. • Both photographs courtesy of film First Freedom. Photographer, Mark Mabry.

more than eleven thousand signed petitions in opposition to Henry's assessment to support Christianity. The measure failed, and the following year Virginia adopted Jefferson's *Statute for Religious Freedom,* which ensured that "no man shall be compelled to frequent or support any religious worship, place, or ministry whatsoever" and promised that "all men shall be free to profess, and by argument to maintain, their opinions in matters of religion."[59]

Years later, looking back on a remarkable career that included stints as member of the House of Burgesses and the Continental Congress, governor of Virginia, drafter of the Declaration of Independence, secretary of state, founder of the University of Virginia, and two terms as president of the United States, Jefferson numbered the passage of the Virginia Statute for Religious Freedom among his most significant achievements.

The Great American Experiment

The American Revolution was an experiment in republicanism, which we would now call *democracy.* Those early Americans knew they were engaging in a grand experiment because there were no great republics in the eighteenth century. There were a few small republics—Venice and some Italian city-states—but nothing like the sprawling nation that the Americans would create in 1776 in a world otherwise dominated by monarchy. Monarchy had existed from the beginning of time and it seemed essential to most people. Most believed you needed authoritarian government to rule corrupt people. But here

we were in 1776 creating a huge republic when everyone thought people weren't virtuous enough to sustain such a system of government and that it was bound to fail. England had tried it in the seventeenth century, and it ended up in Oliver Cromwell's dictatorship. People believed it would never work. So it was an experiment. Could it sustain itself? That was what Lincoln referred to in his Gettysburg Address

AN APPEAL TO HEAVEN

in the middle of the nineteenth century when the world was again full of monarchs. By then the French republic had gone sour. So it was always an experiment. Could it survive? We were the last best hope. That was built into our consciousness, into our American culture, right from the outset.

GORDON WOOD

Inset: The Liberty Tree Flag, with the motto "Appeal To Heaven" from John Locke's work, Two Treatises of Government. The phrase connotes that after all other alternatives of seeking justice have been exhausted, only an "appeal to heaven" remains. The flag was originally used by a squadron of six cruisers commissioned under George Washington's authority in October 1775. It was established as the flag of the Massachusetts state navy on July 26, 1776.

CHAPTER

6

A
CONSTITUTION
Without GOD

The notion of a christian Commonwealth,
should be exploded forever. . . .
If all the souls in a government were saints of God,
should they be formed into a society by law,
that society could not be a gospel church,
but a creature of state.

— JOHN LELAND —
"A Chronicle of His Time in Virginia" (1790)

ITHIN A FEW SHORT YEARS AFTER IT HAD BEEN FORMED, THE UNITED STATES OF AMERICA WAS ON THE BRINK OF FAILURE. The former colonies were united only loosely under the Articles of Confederation; the federal government could neither pay its debts nor protect its people. Something had to be done. In the summer of 1787, delegates from twelve of the thirteen states gathered in Philadelphia.

James Madison arrived from Virginia eleven days before the meeting was scheduled to begin. Preparation was essential because Madison wanted the Virginia delegation to present an ambitious plan to the Constitutional Convention. Instead of fixing the broken government, the assembly would create an entirely new system. They would create a constitution.

The United States Constitution had a long, difficult nativity: four months of wrangling, compromise, and distrust. So much of Madison's original plan was jettisoned that he became bitterly disappointed. The assembly was on the

Previous Page: Thomas Jefferson cut up and pasted select verses from the Bible to make up what was later dubbed "the Jefferson Bible."

Right: James Madison arrived two weeks early to prepare for the Constitutional Convention, which convened in September 1787 at Independence Hall in Philadelphia.

Courtesy of film First Freedom. Photographer, Mark Mabry.

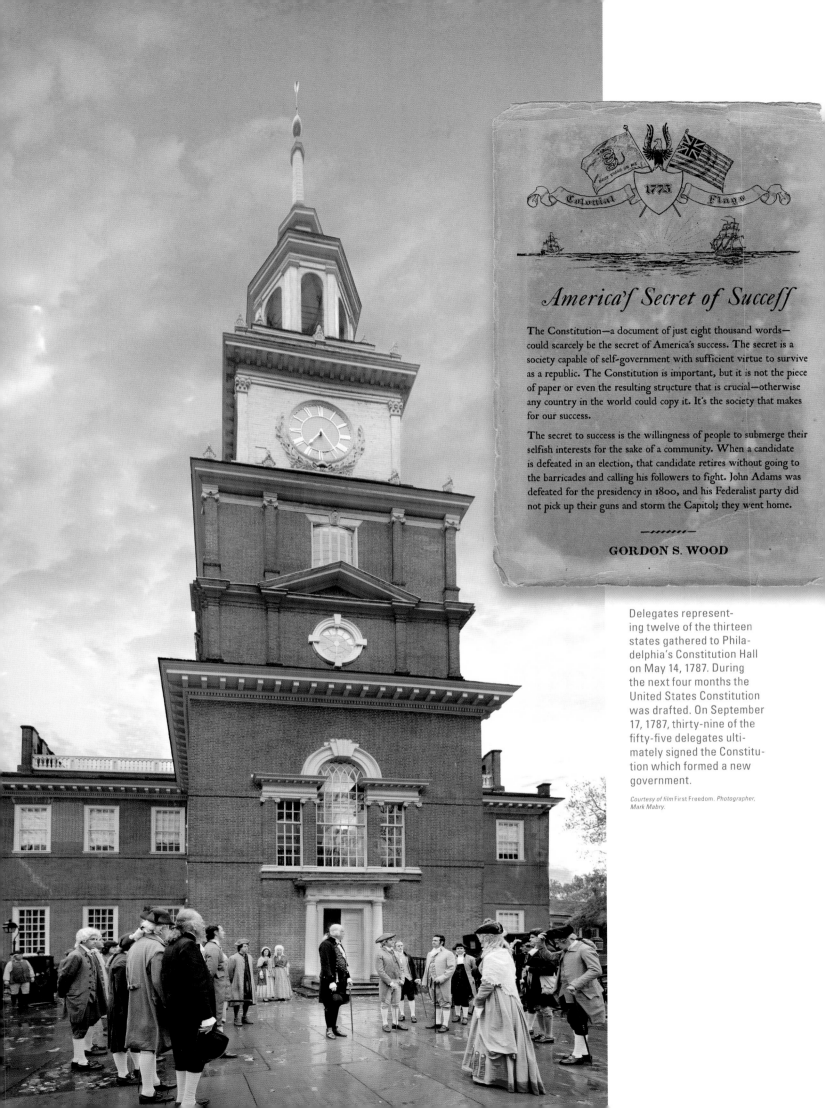

America's Secret of Success

The Constitution—a document of just eight thousand words—could scarcely be the secret of America's success. The secret is a society capable of self-government with sufficient virtue to survive as a republic. The Constitution is important, but it is not the piece of paper or even the resulting structure that is crucial—otherwise any country in the world could copy it. It's the society that makes for our success.

The secret to success is the willingness of people to submerge their selfish interests for the sake of a community. When a candidate is defeated in an election, that candidate retires without going to the barricades and calling his followers to fight. John Adams was defeated for the presidency in 1800, and his Federalist party did not pick up their guns and storm the Capitol; they went home.

GORDON S. WOOD

Delegates representing twelve of the thirteen states gathered to Philadelphia's Constitution Hall on May 14, 1787. During the next four months the United States Constitution was drafted. On September 17, 1787, thirty-nine of the fifty-five delegates ultimately signed the Constitution which formed a new government.

Courtesy of film First Freedom. Photographer, Mark Mabry.

Religious Forces in the Declaration and the Constitution

The foundational documents of the American experiment, the Declaration of Independence and the Constitution, can't be read in isolation one from another. The Declaration is founded on the idea that there is a Creator, a God who has created the world and endowed all of us with certain inalienable rights. Therefore, those rights are sacred. They cannot be tampered with by either the mob or the king. On the other hand, except for prohibiting a religious task for federal office, the only other reference to religion in the original Constitution is a utilitarian one: "The year of our Lord 1787." I think you need both because, in fact, we don't have a godless Constitution.

I also don't think it is impossible to be a Christian nation. We were a nation that was attempting to find ways to respect the rights of believers to pursue their religious lives in as free a context as possible, knowing that those religious values would be brought to the public arena—just as any personal value is going to find expression in the government and in politics. But the Constitution determined how to manage that process—and I don't think there has ever been a better achievement anywhere in the world of both affirming and asserting. The Declaration asserts and affirms that religion is a force in the lives of men—that we are created, that we are endowed by that Creator with certain rights, and that nobody can tamper with them. The Constitution asserts and affirms that we are going to be rational and even-handed about the role of religion in society—in the same way we are rational and even-handed about the role of economics or geography or partisanship in our society. Taken together, they are the two wings on which we rose to the heights we now occupy.

INDEPENDENCE HALL (STATE HOUSE),
PHILADELPHIA, 1774
Dover Publications.

——————

JON MEACHAM

Religious Diversity and the Constitution

The Constitution is interesting because it has virtually no words about religion at all anywhere in it. The Constitution is a remarkably secular document that places government in the hands of the people. The only place we get some words about religion is in the First Amendment. And I think it's significant that the First Amendment deals with freedom of speech and freedom of religion, both of which were seen by the founding fathers as critical to the future of a virtuous society. You can't have a thoughtful, intellectual government if ideas can't be freely circulated. And most of the founding fathers thought religion needed to be given its place, divorced from government and divorced from the state. Such a philosophy freed religion to exercise whatever influence it wanted to within society and gave individuals the power to organize religion for themselves instead of having religion organized by the government.

——————

JON BUTLER

The BRILLIANCE of the DECLARATION and the CONSTITUTION

This country is so enormous and so diverse in ethnicity and origin and religion that the brilliance of the Declaration of Independence, the Constitution, and the Bill of Rights is really overwhelming to me. They are the documents that hold us together as a country. The fact that they recognized that diversity even then is something unusual all by itself. By writing those documents, they managed to find a way to allow us to be diverse and still be one. Those documents capture our unifying—our glue, the things that make us a country, the things that allow us to be different in all kinds of ways without being at war with each other.

——————

COKIE ROBERTS

verge of breaking apart. The only one who could not be discouraged was Benjamin Franklin, now eighty-one years old. Not known for his public speaking, much less for his piety, Franklin offered his suggestion that each day's session of the Constitutional Convention open with prayer.

The delegates rejected Franklin's proposal. As the delegates pulled together, however, and set their minds to the task at hand, they began to fashion a remarkably secular document to be the Constitution of the United States. The muses for the framers of the Constitution were James Harrington, Algernon Sidney, and John Locke, not St. Paul, St. Augustine, or John Calvin. In the original draft of the Constitution, a reference to religion appeared only once. At the insistence of Charles Pinckney of South Carolina, Article VI included the provision that "no religious Test shall ever be required as a Qualification to any Office or public Trust under the United States." The entire document included no reference whatsoever to God. Instead, the Constitution declared itself "the supreme Law of the Land."

Why the aversion to religion? Once again, pluralism played a central role. The framers of the Constitution were well aware of the new nation's religious diversity, and any provision that seemed to favor one species of religious expression over another might imperil ratification of the Constitution.

Above: At eighty-one, Benjamin Franklin was the oldest delegate at the Constitutional Convention.

Inset: Charles Pinckney, 1757–1824.

Courtesy of film First Freedom. *Photographer, Mark Mabry. • Captain Charles Pinckney. Engraved by Charles Balthazar Julien Fevret de, 1770-1852. Published in Ellen G. Miles,* Saint-Mèmin and the Neoclassical Profile Portrait in America. *Washington, DC: National Portrait Gallery, 1994, no. 657. Library of Congress.*

Like any document forged out of political compromise, the Constitution did not please everyone. Franklin lamented that it did not outlaw slavery, although that would have been a deal-breaker for representatives from the South. Some delegates very much supported George Mason's proposal for the inclusion of a bill of rights. Still, the delegates looked upon their work with satisfaction. "I doubt whether any other Convention we can obtain may be able to make a better Constitution," James Wilson declared on behalf of Franklin. "For when you assemble a number of men to have the advantage of their joint wisdom, you inevitably assemble with those men, all their prejudices, their passions, their errors of opinion, their local interests, and their selfish views." Given the vagaries of human nature, Wilson continued, "It therefore astonishes me, Sir, to find this system approaching so near to perfection as it does."[60]

Moments later, all but three of the delegates signed the Constitution. After its passage, even the disappointed James Madison began to look approvingly on the document. Many of the ideas in the Constitution had been his work, but he now pointed toward a different author, crediting "a finger of that Almighty hand which has been so frequently and signally extended to our relief in the critical states of the revolution."[61]

The Constitution then went to the respective states for ratification, where it still faced an uncertain future. A robust debate over the merits of discarding the Articles of Confederation in favor of the proposed Constitution broke out in newspapers, various public forums, street corners, and village greens. The pledge on the part of the Federalists to add a bill of rights allayed fears of a centralized government that might be too strong or too intrusive. With the approval of New Hampshire on June 21, 1788, the Constitution of the United States of America was ratified; the key, and contested, states of Virginia and New York assented soon thereafter. George Washington took the oath of office as president on April 30, 1789.

Washington, who was not a devout man, tried to remain as neutral as possible on matters of religion, worrying

The Articles of Confederation, drafted in 1776 and ultimately ratified by all thirteen colonies, was the working document for the Continental Congress by which the colonies were governed. It also governed the efforts of the Revolutionary War. In 1789 it was replaced by the U. S. Constitution, which allowed a stronger federal government with a chief executive, a court, and a system for taxing the people.

Courtesy of of the Superintendent of Documents, U.S. Government Printing Office. Public domain in the United States because it is a work prepared by an officer or employee of the United States government as part of that person's official duties under the terms of Title 17, Chapter 1, Section 105 of the US Code.

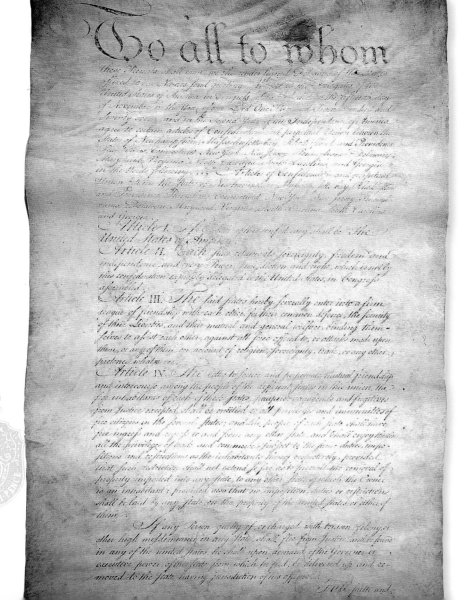

Top: James Wilson, a Scottish immigrant and fellow delegate to the Constitutional Convention, was asked by Benjamin Franklin to read his prepared speech to the assembly. After four months of wrangling, the speech seemed to be the catalyst that brought the delegates to consensus. The Constitution was approved shortly thereafter.

Below: George Washington giving his inaugural speech after taking the presidential oath as the first president of the United States of America.

Courtesy of film First Freedom. *Photographer, Mark Mabry.* • *Unknown artist, circa 1899; courtesy of Prints and Photographs Division, Library of Congress.*

at times that too much religious factionalism imperiled the social order. "Of all the animosities which have existed among mankind, those which are caused by difference of sentiments in religion appear to be the most inveterate and distressing, and ought most to be deprecated," the president wrote in 1792. "I was in hopes that the enlightened and liberal policy, which has marked the present age, would at least have reconciled Christians of every denomination so far that we should never again see the religious disputes carried to such a pitch as to endanger the peace of society."[62]

Despite his relative lack of piety, however, Washington understood the importance of religious freedom. "The citizens of the United States of America have the right to applaud themselves for having given to mankind examples of an enlarged and liberal policy worthy of imitation," he wrote to members of Touro Synagogue in Newport, Rhode

Island. "It is now no more that toleration is spoken of as if it were by the indulgence of one class of citizens that another enjoyed the exercise of their inherent natural rights, for happily the Government of the United States, which gives to bigotry no sanction, to persecution no assistance, requires only that they who live under its protection should demean themselves as good citizens."[63]

Despite Washington's straightforward and eloquent assurances, such guarantees of religious freedom were not yet included in the Constitution itself. What if Washington's successor as president were less tolerant? What if one religious group or another somehow mustered the political influence to have itself declared—and supported with taxpayer funds—as the established religion of the United States? What guarantees did members of minority religions, or no religion at all, have that they would not be taxed to support a national church?

Although James Madison had opposed the inclusion of a bill of rights—he feared than any right *not* specified could someday be denied—political pressure from the Baptists and from Patrick Henry and George Mason forced him to relent. Ultimately, he did not want to entrust the enterprise of formulating a bill of rights to others, so he turned to the task of what he called this "nauseating business of amendments." He also wanted to ensure that the new nation would not move in the direction of established religion. "Ecclesiastical Establishments tend to great ignorance

Background image: George Washington, according to historians, was not outwardly religious, but regularly attended his Episcopal parish at Christ Church in Alexandria, Virginia, when he was at home at Mt. Vernon.

Insets: George Washington and his wife, Martha, with his Book of Common Prayer at Christ Church.

Courtesy of film First Freedom. *Photographer, Mark Mabry.*

Right: Letter from Washington to Touro Synagogue. Below: Letter from Moses Sexias. President George Washington's response to the members of Yeshuat Israel, in Newport Rhode Island, was indicative of his generous and open-minded approach to welcoming people of all faiths in America.

Images of original letters at the Library of Congress—George Washington Papers at the Library of Congress, 1741–1799: Series 2 Letterbooks.

AMERICAN JEWS & RELIGIOUS LIBERTY

In 1790, when that letter was written, there were about 3,000 Jews in all of the colonies. For a letter to assure that there would be no approbation whatsoever of any kind of discrimination or persecution against the Jewish community had to have been tremendously reassuring. The letter was prescient, because it was looking way ahead in terms of what this country has come to stand for in terms of religious freedom. And yet it was very much of the moment as it reassured this small community, a community that probably felt very vulnerable. And that reassurance came from the top—from President Washington himself.

—————

DANIEL MASIASCHIN

The Constitution of the United States of America.

United States; If he approve he shall sign it, but if not he shall return it, with his Objections to that House in which it shall have originated, who shall enter the Objections at large on their Journal, and proceed to reconsider it. If after such Reconsideration two thirds of that House shall agree to pass the Bill, it shall be sent, together with the Objections, to the other House, by which it shall likewise be reconsidered, and if approved by two thirds of that House, it shall become a Law. But in all such Cases the Votes of both Houses shall be determined by yeas and Nays, and the Names of the Persons voting for and against the Bill shall be entered on the Journal of each House respectively. If any Bill shall not be returned by the President within ten Days (Sundays excepted) after it shall have been presented to him, the Same shall be a Law, in like Manner as if he had signed it, unless the Congress by their Adjournment prevent its Return, in which Case it shall not be a Law.

Every Order, Resolution, or Vote to which the Concurrence of the Senate and House of Representatives may be necessary (except on a question of Adjournment) shall be presented to the President of the United States; and before the Same shall take Effect, shall be approved by him, or being disapproved by him, shall be repassed by two thirds of the Senate and House of Representatives, according to the Rules and Limitations prescribed in the Case of a Bill.

Section. 8. The Congress shall have Power To lay and collect Taxes, Duties, Imposts and Excises, to pay the Debts and provide for the common Defence and general Welfare of the United States; but all Duties, Imposts and Excises shall be uniform throughout the United States;

To borrow Money on the credit of the United States;

To regulate Commerce with foreign Nations, and among the several States, and with the Indian Tribes;

To establish an uniform Rule of Naturalization, and uniform Laws on the subject of Bankruptcies throughout the United States;

To coin Money, regulate the Value thereof, and of foreign Coin, and fix the Standard of Weights and Measures;

To provide for the Punishment of counterfeiting the Securities and current Coin of the United States;

To establish Post Offices and post Roads;

To promote the Progress of Science and useful Arts, by securing for limited Times to Authors and Inventors the exclusive Right to their respective Writings and Discoveries;

To constitute Tribunals inferior to the supreme Court;

To define and punish Piracies and Felonies committed on the high Seas, and Offences against the Law of Nations;

To declare War, grant Letters of Marque and Reprisal, and make Rules concerning Captures on Land and Water;

To raise and support Armies, but no Appropriation of Money to that Use shall be for a longer Term than two Years;

To provide and maintain a Navy;

To make Rules for the Government and Regulation of the land and naval Forces;

To provide for calling forth the Militia to execute the Laws of the Union, suppress Insurrections and repel Invasions;

To provide for organizing, arming, and disciplining, the Militia, and for governing such Part of them as may be employed in the Service of the United States, reserving to the States respectively, the Appointment of the Officers, and the Authority of training the Militia according to the discipline prescribed by Congress;

To exercise exclusive Legislation in all Cases whatsoever, over such District (not exceeding ten Miles square) as may, by Cession of particular States, and the Acceptance of Congress, become the Seat of the Government of the United States, and to exercise like Authority over all Places purchased by the Consent of the Legislature of the State in which the Same shall be, for the Erection of Forts, Magazines, Arsenals, dock-Yards, and other needful Buildings;—— And

To make all Laws which shall be necessary and proper for carrying into Execution the foregoing Powers, and all other Powers vested by this Constitution in the Government of the United States, or in any Department or Officer thereof.

Section. 9. The Migration or Importation of such Persons as any of the States now existing shall think proper to admit, shall not be prohibited by the Congress prior to the Year one thousand eight hundred and eight, but a Tax or duty may be imposed on such Importation, not exceeding ten dollars for each Person.

The Privilege of the Writ of Habeas Corpus shall not be suspended, unless when in Cases of Rebellion or Invasion the public Safety may require it.

No Bill of Attainder or ex post facto Law shall be passed.

No Capitation, or other direct, Tax shall be laid, unless in Proportion to the Census or Enumeration herein before directed to be taken.

No Tax or Duty shall be laid on Articles exported from any State.

No Preference shall be given by any Regulation of Commerce or Revenue to the Ports of one State over those of another: nor shall Vessels bound to, or from, one State, be obliged to enter, clear, or pay Duties in another.

No Money shall be drawn from the Treasury, but in Consequence of Appropriations made by Law; and a regular Statement and Account of the Receipts and Expenditures of all public Money shall be published from time to time.

No Title of Nobility shall be granted by the United States: And no Person holding any Office of Profit or Trust under them, shall, without the Consent of the Congress, accept of any present, Emolument, Office, or Title, of any kind whatever, from any King, Prince, or foreign State.

Section. 10. No State shall enter into any Treaty, Alliance, or Confederation; grant Letters of Marque and Reprisal; coin Money; emit Bills of Credit; make any Thing but gold and silver Coin a Tender in Payment of Debts; pass any Bill of Attainder, ex post facto Law, or Law impairing the Obligation of Contracts, or grant any Title of Nobility.

No State shall, without the Consent of the Congress, lay any Imposts or Duties on Imports or Exports, except what may be absolutely necessary for executing its inspection Laws: and the net Produce of all Duties and Imposts, laid by any State on Imports or Exports, shall be for the Use of the Treasury of the United States; and all such Laws shall be subject to the Revision and Controul of the Congress.

No State shall, without the Consent of Congress, lay any Duty of Tonnage, keep Troops, or Ships of War in time of Peace, enter into any Agreement or Compact with another State, or with a foreign Power, or engage in War, unless actually invaded, or in such imminent Danger as will not admit of delay.

Article. II.

Section. 1. The executive Power shall be vested in a President of the United States of America. He shall hold his Office during the Term of four Years, and, together with the Vice President, chosen for the same Term, be elected, as follows.

Each State shall appoint, in such Manner as the Legislature thereof may direct, a Number of Electors, equal to the whole Number of Senators and Representatives to which the State may be entitled in the Congress: but no Senator or Representative, or Person holding an Office of Trust or Profit under the United States, shall be appointed an Elector.

The Electors shall meet in their respective States, and vote by Ballot for two Persons, of whom one at least shall not be an Inhabitant of the same the same State with themselves. And they shall make a List of all the Persons voted for, and of the Number of Votes for each; which List they shall sign and certify, and transmit sealed to the Seat of the Government of the United States, directed to the President of the Senate. The President of the Senate shall in the Presence of the Senate and House of Representatives, open all the Certificates, and the Votes shall then be counted. The Person having the greatest Number of Votes shall be the President, if such Number be a Majority of the whole Number of Electors appointed; and if there be more than one who have such Majority, and have an equal Number of Votes, then the House of Representatives shall immediately chuse by Ballot one of them for President; and if no Person have a Majority, then from the five highest on the List the said House shall in like Manner chuse the President. But in chusing the President, the Votes shall be taken by States, the Representation from each State having one Vote; A quorum for this Purpose shall consist of a Member or Members from two thirds of the States, and a Majority of all the States shall be necessary to a Choice. In every Case, after the Choice of the President, the Person having the greatest Number of Votes of the Electors shall be the Vice President. But if there should remain two or more who have equal Votes, the Senate shall chuse from them by Ballot the Vice President.

The Congress may determine the Time of chusing the Electors, and the Day on which they shall give their Votes; which Day shall be the same throughout the United States.

No Person except a natural born Citizen, or a Citizen of the United States, at the time of the Adoption of this Constitution, shall be eligible to the Office of President; neither shall any Person be eligible to that Office who shall not have attained to the Age of thirty five Years, and been fourteen Years a Resident within the United States.

In Case of the Removal of the President from Office, or of his Death, Resignation, or Inability to discharge the Powers and Duties of the said Office, the same shall devolve on the Vice President, and the Congress may by Law provide for the Case of Removal, Death, Resignation or Inability, both of the President and Vice President, declaring what Officer shall then act as President, and such Officer shall act accordingly, until the Disability be removed, or a President shall be elected.

The President shall, at stated Times, receive for his Services, a Compensation, which shall neither be encreased nor diminished during the Period for which he shall have been elected, and he shall not receive within that Period any other Emolument from the United States, or any of them.

Before he enter on the Execution of his Office, he shall take the following Oath or Affirmation:— "I do solemnly swear (or affirm) that I will faithfully execute the Office of President of the United States, and will to the best of my Ability, preserve, protect and defend the Constitution of the United States."

Section. 2. The President shall be Commander in Chief of the Army and Navy of the United States, and of the Militia of the several States, when called into the actual Service of the United States; he may require the Opinion, in writing, of the principal Officer in each of the executive Departments, upon any Subject relating to the Duties of their respective Offices, and he shall have Power to grant Reprieves and Pardons for Offences against the United States, except in Cases of Impeachment.

He shall have Power, by and with the Advice and Consent of the Senate, to make Treaties, provided two thirds of the Senators present concur; and he shall nominate, and by and with the Advice and Consent of the Senate, shall appoint Ambassadors, other public Ministers and Consuls, Judges of the supreme Court, and all other Officers of the United States, whose Appointments are not herein otherwise provided for, and which shall be established by Law: but the Congress may by Law vest the Appointment of such inferior Officers, as they think proper, in the President alone, in the Courts of Law, or in the Heads of Departments.

The President shall have Power to fill up all Vacancies that may happen during the Recess of the Senate, by granting Commissions which shall expire at the End of their next Session.

Section. 3. He shall from time to time give to the Congress Information of the State of the Union, and recommend to their Consideration such Measures as he shall judge necessary and expedient; he may, on extraordinary Occasions, convene both Houses, or either of them, and in Case of Disagreement between them, with Respect to the Time of Adjournment, he may adjourn them to such Time as he shall think proper; he shall receive Ambassadors and other public Ministers; he shall take Care that the Laws be faithfully executed, and shall Commission all the Officers of the United States.

Section. 4. The President, Vice President and all civil Officers of the United States, shall be removed from Office on Impeachment for, and Conviction of, Treason, Bribery, or other high Crimes and Misdemeanors.

Article III.

Section. 1. The judicial Power of the United States, shall be vested in one supreme Court, and in such inferior Courts as the Congress may from time to time ordain and establish. The Judges, both of the supreme and inferior Courts, shall hold their Offices during good Behaviour, and shall, at stated Times, receive for their Services, a Compensation, which shall not be diminished during their Continuance in Office.

Section. 2. The judicial Power shall extend to all Cases, in Law and Equity, arising under this Constitution, the Laws of the United States, and Treaties made, or which shall be made, under their Authority;— to all Cases affecting Ambassadors, other public Ministers and Consuls;— to all Cases of admiralty and maritime Jurisdiction;— to Controversies to which the United States shall be a Party;— to Controversies between two or more States;— between a State and Citizens of another State;— between Citizens of different States,— between Citizens of the same State claiming Lands under Grants of different States, and between a State, or the Citizens thereof, and foreign States, Citizens or Subjects.

In all Cases affecting Ambassadors, other public Ministers and Consuls, and those in which a State shall be Party, the supreme Court shall have original Jurisdiction. In all the other Cases before mentioned, the supreme Court shall have appellate Jurisdiction, both as to Law and Fact, with such Exceptions, and under such Regulations as the Congress shall make.

The Trial of all Crimes, except in Cases of Impeachment, shall be by Jury; and such Trial shall be held in the State where the said Crimes shall have been committed; but when not committed within any State, the Trial shall be at such Place or Places as the Congress may by Law have directed.

Section. 3. Treason against the United States, shall consist only in levying War against them, or in adhering to their Enemies, giving them Aid and Comfort. No Person shall be convicted of Treason unless on the Testimony of two Witnesses to the same overt Act, or on Confession in open Court.

The Congress shall have Power to declare the Punishment of Treason, but no Attainder of Treason shall work Corruption of Blood, or Forfeiture except during the Life of the Person attainted.

Article IV.

Section. 1. Full Faith and Credit shall be given in each State to the public Acts, Records, and judicial Proceedings of every other State. And the

Congress may by general Laws prescribe the Manner in which such Acts, Records and Proceedings shall be proved, and the Effect thereof.

Section. 2. The Citizens of each State shall be entitled to all Privileges and Immunities of Citizens in the several States.

A Person charged in any State with Treason, Felony, or other Crime, who shall flee from Justice, and be found in another State, shall on Demand of the executive Authority of the State from which he fled, be delivered up, to be removed to the State having Jurisdiction of the Crime.

No Person held to Service or Labour in one State, under the Laws thereof, escaping into another, shall, in Consequence of any Law or Regulation therein, be discharged from such Service or Labour, but shall be delivered up on Claim of the Party to whom such Service or Labour may be due.

Section. 3. New States may be admitted by the Congress into this Union; but no new State shall be formed or erected within the Jurisdiction of any other State; nor any State be formed by the Junction of two or more States, or Parts of States, without the Consent of the Legislatures of the States concerned as well as of the Congress.

The Congress shall have Power to dispose of and make all needful Rules and Regulations respecting the Territory or other Property belonging to the United States; and nothing in this Constitution shall be so construed as to Prejudice any Claims of the United States, or of any particular State.

Section. 4. The United States shall guarantee to every State in this Union a Republican Form of Government, and shall protect each of them against Invasion; and on Application of the Legislature, or of the Executive (when the Legislature cannot be convened) against domestic Violence.

Article. V.

The Congress, whenever two thirds of both Houses shall deem it necessary, shall propose Amendments to this Constitution, or, on the Application of the Legislatures of two thirds of the several States, shall call a Convention for proposing Amendments, which, in either Case, shall be valid to all Intents and Purposes, as Part of this Constitution, when ratified by the Legislatures of three fourths of the several States, or by Conventions in three fourths thereof, as the one or the other Mode of Ratification may be proposed by the Congress; Provided that no Amendment which may be made prior to the Year One thousand eight hundred and eight shall in any Manner affect the first and fourth Clauses in the Ninth Section of the first Article; and that no State, without its Consent, shall be deprived of its equal Suffrage in the Senate.

Article. VI.

All Debts contracted and Engagements entered into, before the Adoption of this Constitution, shall be as valid against the United States under this Constitution, as under the Confederation.

This Constitution, and the Laws of the United States which shall be made in Pursuance thereof; and all Treaties made, or which shall be made, under the Authority of the United States, shall be the supreme Law of the Land; and the Judges in every State shall be bound thereby, any Thing in the Constitution or Laws of any State to the Contrary notwithstanding.

The Senators and Representatives before mentioned, and the Members of the several State Legislatures, and all executive and judicial Officers, both of the United States and of the several States, shall be bound by Oath or Affirmation, to support this Constitution; but no religious Test shall ever be required as a Qualification to any Office or public Trust under the United States.

Article. VII.

The Ratification of the Conventions of nine States, shall be sufficient for the Establishment of this Constitution between the States so ratifying the Same.

The Word "the" being interlined between the seventh and eighth Lines of the first Page, The Word "Thirty" being partly written on an Erazure in the fifteenth Line of the first Page. The words "is tried" being interlined between the thirty second and thirty third Lines of the first Page and the Word "the" being interlined between the forty third and forty fourth Lines of the second Page.

Attest William Jackson Secretary

done in Convention by the Unanimous Consent of the States present the Seventeenth Day of September in the Year of our Lord one thousand seven hundred and Eighty seven and of the Independance of the United States of America the Twelfth In Witness whereof We have hereunto subscribed our Names,

Go. Washington—Presidt. and deputy from Virginia

Delaware
Geo: Read
Gunning Bedford jun
John Dickinson
Richard Bassett
Jaco: Broom

Maryland
James McHenry
Dan of St Thos. Jenifer
Danl Carroll

Virginia
John Blair—
James Madison Jr.

North Carolina
Wm. Blount
Richd. Dobbs Spaight.
Hu Williamson

South Carolina
J. Rutledge
Charles Cotesworth Pinckney
Charles Pinckney
Pierce Butler.

Georgia
William Few
Abr Baldwin

New Hampshire
John Langdon
Nicholas Gilman

Massachusetts
Nathaniel Gorham
Rufus King

Connecticut
Wm. Saml. Johnson
Roger Sherman

New York
Alexander Hamilton

New Jersey
Wil: Livingston
David Brearley
Wm. Paterson
Jona: Dayton

Pennsylvania
B Franklin
Thomas Mifflin
Robt. Morris
Geo. Clymer
Thos. FitzSimons
Jared Ingersoll
James Wilson
Gouv Morris

The Need for a
VIRTUOUS SOCIETY

Public virtue is at the heart of the American Revolution and was in the eyes and in the minds of the revolutionaries. That virtue meant self-sacrifice, patriotism, and willingness to give up selfish interests for the sake of a larger good. So it was crucial that the republic—really a form of self-government— to be made up of people with lots of virtue. They couldn't be compelled from above to be ruled, curbed, or commanded. They had to willingly give up their selfish interests for the sake of their community. So it became very essential that, as political scientists of the eighteenth century maintained, "Republics require—absolutely require, virtue in their people. Otherwise it won't hold together."

John Adams was probably one of the more cynical of the founders; he and Alexander Hamilton had constant doubts about the virtuous quality of the American people. At the other end of the spectrum was Thomas Jefferson, who had a very magnanimous view of human nature, who believed that people were essentially virtuous, and who believed that the Revolution could be sustained. That's why he believed in minimal government—he didn't think we needed to be governed from the top down and that we were capable of somehow voluntarily merging our private interests into the collective.

The view of human nature is what separates one founder from another. George Washington would have been on the realist end with Hamilton and Adams. He said, "It would be wonderful if people weren't selfish, if they didn't have self- interests to promote but unfortunately that is the way of the world." He adopted that realist position and worked from there. He didn't go so far as advocating monarchy; he was a good Republican in that sense. But he had certain doubts about what he would have called the Utopian view—that we don't need government to command and control us.

— ///// —

GORDON S. WOOD

Virtue In The New American Society

The idea of virtue was absolutely essential to the theory of democracy. In a monarchy, the responsibility for government rests on the king. He enforces the laws through his executors of the law. But in a democracy the people are sovereign; if they are not virtuous, chaos results. For the colonists, the only way to virtue was through religion. So it was almost impossible to conceive of a democracy that didn't have a strong religious element.

— ///// —

RICHARD BUSHMAN

Inset: Boston's Faneuil Hall has been called "the cradle of American liberty," having been the popular gathering place of the Sons of Liberty during the incipient stages of the Revolution. Benson J. Lossing, The Pictorial Field-Book of the Revolution (New York: Harper & Brothers, 1851)I:479. Florida Center for Instructional Technology, College of Education, University of South Florida. • Background photo: Courtesy of film First Freedom. Photography, Mark Mabry.

A Truly
REMARKABLE DOCUMENT

The Constitution was driven by perceptions of very serious problems for an early republic with an extraordinarily shaky foundation of thirteen separate states. Who was going to conduct foreign policy? Who was going to establish a currency? Who was going to create a working government? Add to that the driving concern about whether it was right or wrong. It was possible the old Articles of Confederation could have worked, but many thought that they weren't working and that the chance of them working in the future was even dimmer.

Through a series of extraordinary circumstances, the United States was blessed with an extraordinary set of political leaders; it could be said that the likes of them had never been seen before or since. They were extraordinarily intelligent, they were widely read, and they were philosophical in a general sense. But they were also very pragmatic in the sense that they wanted to apply their philosophical understandings to the problems of their own day with intelligence and sophistication—and with a sense to the future.

They were informed by the past but they weren't driven by the past or fearful of the past. They weren't as partisan as Americans have often been since. They were willing to grant that someone else had a good idea even if it wasn't their idea. And in that regard the Constitution was a document for all times by men for all times, and it's rare that one sees that in the founding moments of a society. But, in fact, that's exactly what happened in America—and the result was the creation of a truly remarkable document.

— ///// —

JON BUTLER

Riots broke out among some of the smaller religious groups when President John Adams announced a national day of fasting; however, he was not the first to establish such a proclamaiton. On June 12, 1775, the First Continental Congress issued a proclamation for a national day of "Fasting, Humiliation and Prayer" to be held on July 20, setting the precedent for future proclamations. In 1779 Congress set the first Thursday in May as a day of "Fasting, Humiliation and Prayer to Almighty God." Congress urged Americans to "confess and bewail our manifold sins and transgressions, and by a sincere repentance and amendment of life, appease his [God's] righteous displeasure, and through the merits and mediation of Jesus Christ, obtain his pardon and forgiveness." President George Washington later declared February 19, 1795, a day for prayer and public thanksgiving.

E. Benjamin Andrews, History of the United States from the Earliest Discovery of American to the Present Day (New York: Charles Scribner's Sons, 1895), 2:37. Florida Center for Instructional Technology, College of Education, University of South Florida. • Fast Day Proclamation, March 23, 1798. John Adams. Broadside. Rare Book and Special Collections Division, Library of Congress.

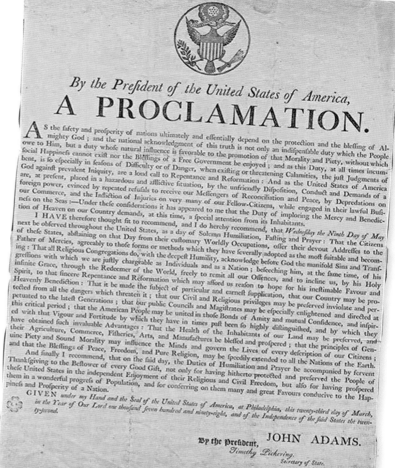

and Corruption," Madison had written to William Bradford Jr. in 1774, "all of which facilitate the Execution of mischievous Projects."[64]

What flowed from Madison's pen, as amended by the Senate and the House of Representatives, was a triumph—sixteen words in spare prose that set a new course for religion and politics, church and state: "Congress shall make no law respecting an establishment of religion, or prohibiting the free exercise thereof." For perhaps the first time in history, especially in the West, a government pledged to stay out of the religion business, simultaneously guaranteeing both free exercise of religion and freedom from established religion.

The new the Bill of Rights, like the Constitution itself, did not please everyone. "Many pious people wish the name of the Supreme Being had been introduced somewhere in the new Constitution," Benjamin Rush had written in 1789. "Perhaps an acknowledgement may be made of his goodness or of his providence in the proposed amendments." In that respect of directly invoking the deity, the Bill of Rights, like the Constitution, disappointed.[65]

The First Amendment applied only to the federal government. Many of the states, notably Connecticut and Massachusetts, continued to support specific denominations with tax money. In Massachusetts, Isaac Backus persisted in his campaign against the Congregational establishment. He recounted the long and tawdry history of religious coercion, noting that "pure Gospel discipline in the church is very little if at all known in state establishments of religion." Backus reminded his fellow citizens that Baptists had "joined as heartily in the general defense of our country as any denomination therein, and I have a better opinion of my countrymen than to think the majority of them will now agree to deny us liberty of conscience." The people of Massachusetts would have to wait until 1833 for the demise of their religious establishment.

On the federal level, some confusion remained about exactly where to draw this line of separation between church and state. What about military chaplains or Congressional chaplains? After he left the White House, James Madison opined that the formation of a Congressional chaplaincy was "a palpable violation of equal rights, as well as of Constitutional principles." The appropriation of public funds to support a chaplain, he believed, represented taxpayer support for religion. "If Religion consist in voluntary acts of individuals, singly, or voluntarily associated," he wrote, "and it be proper that public functionaries, as well as their constituents should discharge their religious duties, let them like their constituents, do so at their own expense."[66]

When John Adams, Washington's successor as president, declared a national day of fasting, riots broke out among some of the smaller religious groups whose members feared that the government was overstepping its bounds. Adams's declaration of two "national fasts" emerged as an issue in the bitter presidential campaign of 1800. His challenger, Thomas Jefferson, opposed the idea of a national fast day. Years later, Adams attributed his defeat in 1800 to the fast days. "The National Fast, recommended by me turned me out of office," he wrote to Benjamin Rush in 1812. The declaration, Adams acknowledged, alienated "Quakers, Anabaptists, Mennonists, Moravians, Swedenborgians, Methodists, Catholicks, protestant Episcopalians, Arians Socinians, Armenians."[67]

Adams had fought Jefferson's charges with charges of his own, namely that Jefferson did not believe in God. If Jefferson were elected, Adams and the Federalists warned, Americans, bereft of religion, would become "more ferocious than savages, more bloody than tigers, more impious than demons."

Inset Left: Benjamin Rush, 1757–1824, lived in the state of Pennsylvania and was one of the founding fathers. Despite his contributions to early American society, Rush may be more famous today as the man who, in 1812, helped reconcile the friendship of Thomas Jefferson and John Adams by encouraging the two former presidents to resume writing to each other.

Below: The election of 1800 between John Adams and Thomas Jefferson was bitter and included printed recriminations. John Adams grew up in the Congregational Church in Braintree, Massachusetts. By the time he wrote this letter, his theological position can best be described as Unitarian. In this letter Adams tells Jefferson that "without Religion this World would be Something not fit to be mentioned in polite Company, I mean Hell."

Benjamin Rush. Engraved by Charles Balthazar Julien Fevret de, 1770-1852. Published in Ellen G. Miles, Saint-Mémin and the Neoclassical Profile Portrait in America. Washington, D.C.: National Portrait Gallery, 1994, no. 657. Library of Congress. • Holograph letter. Manuscript Division, Library of Congress. • Courtesy of film First Freedom. Photographer, Mark Mabry.

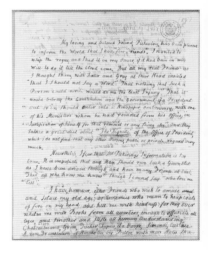

The *Gazette of the United States*, the nation's leading Federalist newspaper, put the matter starkly: "The only question to be asked by every American, laying his hand on his heart, is 'Shall I continue in allegiance to GOD—AND A RELIGIOUS PRESIDENT; or impiously declare for JEFFERSON—AND NO GOD!!!'"[68]

Jefferson's religious views were indeed complicated. Although reared in the Church of England, he was most likely never confirmed. He did serve as member of the vestry, and he provided financial support for various parishes, but Jefferson was a creature of the Enlightenment. He was fascinated by Jesus, though not as the Son of God but as a moral teacher; Jefferson pronounced himself "sincerely attached to his doctrines, in preference to all others; ascribing to himself every human excellence, and believing he never claimed any other."[69]

Jefferson's rationalism would not allow him to believe in miracles, so he excised all references to the supernatural from the New Testament in order to produce the *Jefferson Bible; or, The Life and Morals of Jesus of Nazareth*. "To the corruptions of Christianity I am indeed opposed; but not to the genuine precepts of Jesus himself," Jefferson explained to Benjamin Rush, repeating, "I am a Christian, in the only sense he wished any one to be; sincerely attached to his doctrines, in preference to all others; ascribing to himself every *human* excellence; & believing he never claimed any other."[70]

Jefferson prevailed in the bitter presidential election of 1800. His inauguration on March 4, 1801, marked the first transfer of political power from one party to another in American history. It also vindicated the

Inset Top: Thomas Jefferson created his own Bible by cutting up scriptures from two identical Bibles so that he could have his own version that contained the teachings of Jesus Christ.

Inset Bottom: John Toland (1670–1722) was a leading English Deist. His works, which challenged the heart of orthodox Christian belief, found a following in the American colonies, including with Thomas Jefferson.

What Was Deism?

Deism has many definitions because it was a broad movement. It's always hard to define where an intellectual movement starts and what it encompasses. But there are five classical points of Deism, and that should be the starting basis of what, according to the movement, one should believe.

1—There is a God.

2—That God should be worshipped.

3—Being moral or virtuous is the best way to worship God.

4—We ought to be sorry for our misdoings (note that the word is *misdoings*, not *sins*).

5—There is life after death where the good are rewarded and the evil punished.

Benjamin Franklin received a letter on his deathbed from the president of Yale, who was a Congregationalist minister, asking what Franklin really believed. Franklin answered in a letter that's often quoted and is simply in large part a piecing together of these five points—and it has every one of these five points. Franklin says he is not sure of Jesus' divinity, but he feels he shouldn't check any further into it because he so soon will have the chance to find out first hand. Very prudent man, and an honest statement of his feelings on the five points of Deism. Incidentally, the five points don't mention church, they don't mention synagogue, they don't mention worship, they don't mention sacraments, they don't mention Bar mitzvahs, they don't mention clergy, they don't mention scripture, they don't even mention prayer.

———·//////·———

DAVID L. HOLMES

Chri~~sti~~anity not Mysterious:
OR, A
TREATISE
Shewing,
That there is nothing in the
GOSPEL
Contrary to
REASON,
Nor ABOVE it:
And that no Christian Doctrine can be properly call'd
A MYSTERY.

London, Printed in the Year 1696.

constitutional notion that religion and politics should not be intertwined. "If the freedom of religion, guaranteed to us by law *in theory*, can ever rise *in practice* under the overbearing inquisition of public opinion," Jefferson wrote, "truth will prevail over fanaticism."[71]

Jefferson's ascendance to the presidency demonstrated that religious passions would not interfere with the workings of government. But how did the First Amendment affect religious life in the new nation?

The populism that became a fixture of religious life during the Great Awakening served religious leaders in good stead. The First Amendment set up what was effectively a free marketplace for religion in the United States. No longer could clergy rely on taxpayer support; they had to appeal to the masses. To continue the economic metaphor, religious entrepreneurs began to circulate, selling their wares, seeking popular followings. The most successful religious movements in American history have competed in this free marketplace of American religion, a marketplace unfettered by state interference, where no religion is favored, and none proscribed.

When Adam Smith published his classic treatise on capitalism in 1776, *The Wealth of Nations*, he used religion as an example of the beneficial effects of competition. Benjamin Franklin had expressed a similar sentiment about the benefits of a religious marketplace. "When a Religion is good, I conceive it will support itself," Franklin wrote in 1780, "and when it does not support itself, and God does not take care to support it so that its Professors are obliged to call for help of the Civil Power, it is a sign, I apprehend, of its being a bad one." The First Amendment illustrated the power of the religious marketplace. "There are but two ways of preserving visible religion in any country," Benjamin Rush observed in 1784. "The first is by establishments. The second is by the competition of different religious societies." American history has amply demonstrated the superiority of the latter.[72]

From Monticello, more than a decade after he had left the White House, Thomas Jefferson reflected on the great America experiment of separating church and state. "Our country has been the first to prove to the world two truths, the most salutary to human society, that man can govern himself, and that religious freedom is the most effective anodyne against religious dissension," he wrote. Jefferson pointed out what many Americans, then and now, would regard as a paradox: "The maxims of civil government being reversed in that of religion, where it's [*sic*] true form is 'divided we stand, united we fall.'"[73]

Two years later, James Madison, Jefferson's successor as president, put the matter even more succinctly: "Religion & Govt. will both exist in greater purity, the less they are mixed together."[74]

John Adams (top) died at home in his ninety-first year on July 4, 1826, exactly fifty years after signing the Declaration of Independence. Thomas Jefferson (bottom) died four hours earlier in his eighty-fourth year, also on July 4, 1826. Their deaths marked a coincidental close to the lives of great friends, enemies, and then friends again as they helped to forge the foundation of the government and religious liberty of the United States of America.

Courtesy of film First Freedom. *Photographer, Mark Mabry.*

Epilogue

THE FIRST AMENDMENT MUST HAVE BEEN VERY MUCH ON THOMAS JEFFERSON'S MIND ON NEW YEAR'S DAY, 1802. As he sat down to catch up on his correspondence, the president came across a letter dated October 7 of the previous year and signed by Nehemiah Dodge, Ephram Robbins, and Stephen S. Nelson on behalf of a group of Baptists from Danbury, Connecticut. A year before that, when Jefferson was running against incumbent president John Adams, Jefferson's variance with orthodox opinions was very much an issue, especially among the Federalists in New England, who feared for the loss of Congregationalism as the preferred religion in Connecticut and Massachusetts. In response to the campaign invective directed against Jefferson, Baptists, Presbyterians, and other dissenters had rallied to his defense.

The occasion of the letter from the Baptists in Danbury was to express support for the president's efforts to extend religious disestablishment to the states. "Our sentiments are uni-

formly on the side of religious liberty," the Baptists wrote, "that Religion is at all times and places a matter between God and individuals; that no man ought to suffer in name, person, or effects on account of his religious opinions."[75]

Earlier that same day, Jefferson had received an unusual entourage at the White House. While Jefferson was spending his days at Monticello, he had befriended a Baptist neighbor, John Leland, who became one of Jefferson's most fervent supporters. Leland moved to Cheshire, Massachusetts, in 1792 and continued his ministry among the Baptists there, many of whom had come from Rhode Island. Leland enthusiastically supported Jefferson's election in 1800, rallying the town of Cheshire behind him. Early during Jefferson's first term, Leland sought to demonstrate that not all of New England opposed the Virginian.[76]

The Baptist preacher came up with the idea of presenting the president a local product as a token of their support and affection. Some of the residents of Cheshire, Massachusetts, had come from Cheshire, Connecticut, a town known for its cheese. Leland directed that all of the locals in Cheshire, Massachusetts, collect the milk from their cows on a single day—July 20, 1801—and that they prepare the curds and bring them to the farm of Elisha Brown Jr. Brown's large cider press, with some modification, provided a cheese hoop, four feet in diameter

Previous Page: Thomas Jefferson in his study at Monticello.

Courtesy of film First Freedom. *Photographer, Mark Mabry.*

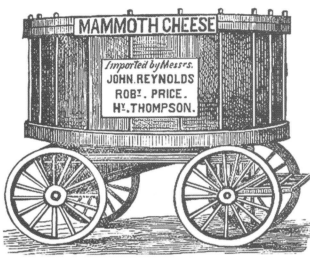

Above: John Leland was an influential Baptist preacher who wrote a letter containing ten objections to the Constitution that he sent to Colonel Thomas Barbour, an opponent of the Constitution in James Madison's Orange County district. Leland's objections were copied by Captain Joseph Spencer, one of Madison's Baptist friends, and sent to Madison so that he could refute the arguments. Leland's final objection was that the new Constitution did not sufficiently secure "What is dearest of all—Religious Liberty." His chief worry was "if a Majority of Congress with the President favour one System more than another, they may oblige all others to pay to the support of their System as much as they please." In the summer of 1801, John Leland asked the ladies of his Baptist congregation to make a large cheese as a gift for President Jefferson in honor of his great achievements and for his support of freedom to practice religion without interference from the government.

From Robert Carlton Brown, The Complete Book of Cheese, *1886–1959.*

and eighteen inches tall. Leland specifically directed that no milk from Federalist cows be allowed, "lest it should leaven the whole lump with a distasteful savour." As the whey was being pressed out of the hoop, Leland blessed the cheese, dedicated it to the nation's chief executive, and led the townspeople in the singing of a hymn.

A month after the pressing, the round of cheese weighed in at 1,235 pounds. Additional curds had been sufficient to produce another three rounds, each weighing 70 pounds. By early December, the "Mammoth Cheese," as it was known, was placed on a sled and carried to Hudson, New York, where it was conveyed by barge first to New York City and then on to Baltimore or Washington (accounts differ). Leland and a friend, Darius Brown, accompanied the cheese, alternately in the same conveyance or by parallel route; Leland, who had long experience as an itinerant minister, preached to audiences along the way.

The December 30, 1801, edition of the *National Intelligencer and Washington Advertiser* recorded the arrival of the Mammoth Cheese: "Yesterday the cheese, made in Massachusetts to be presented to the President, was brought to the city in a wagon drawn by six horses." On the morning of New Year's Day, 1802, Leland presented the cheese to the president "as a token of the esteem

we bear to our chief Magistrate," along with an effusive letter of support from the people of Cheshire, Massachusetts. The declaration included appreciation for the Constitution and its "prohibition of religious tests to prevent all hierarchy."[77]

Later that day, after entertaining members of the cabinet and foreign diplomats with a tasting of the Mammoth Cheese, Jefferson sat down and penned his famous letter to the Danbury Baptists. "I contemplate with solemn reverence," the president wrote, "that act of the whole American people which declared that their legislature would 'make no law respecting an establishment of religion, of prohibiting the free exercise thereof,' thus building a wall of separation between church and state."[78]

This remarkable confluence of events at the White House on January 1, 1802, serves to underscore the uniqueness of the First Amendment to the United States Constitution. Not only was the notion of constructing a government without the interlocking authority of religion utterly unprecedented in Western history but the First Amendment itself was derived from the remarkable alliance between two unlikely camps: secular rationalists like Thomas Jefferson and evangelicals, especially Baptists, like John Leland. The "wall of separation" metaphor itself can be traced to Roger Williams, founder of the Baptist tradition in America, who sought to protect the "garden of the church" from the "wilderness of the world" by means of a "wall of separation." But there can be

The LEGACY of the FOUNDERS

The founders established a republic, a democracy that turned power to the people. In the end it was a nation that said that the people would

come first and that the people would choose their leaders. America took that advice to heart. American Christians have also taken that to heart, so there is this deeply popular strain of religion that sets faith in this country apart from its European counterparts. It is a deeply pluralistic strain in which a lot of new churches are being formed with leaders rising out of nowhere to command significant followings that aren't necessarily ordained by the core institutions of culture. They didn't go to the best universities. They didn't go to the best seminaries. Yet they rise up by virtue of their democratic oratory to command significant following, and that gives religion a deeply popular cast.

—

NATHAN O. HATCH

Declaration of Independence *by John Trumbull. Library of Congress.*

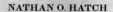

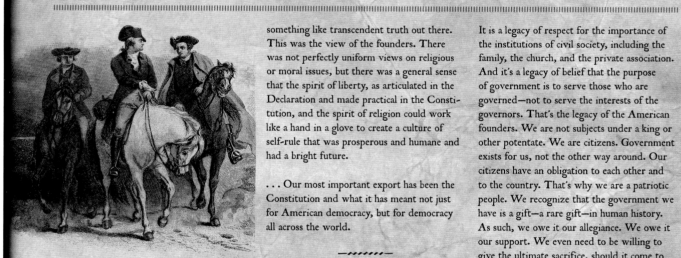

The rich legacy that comes to us from the founders is not contained in a single document. It is not found in a particular law. It is a rich combination of the original Constitution, the Bill of Rights, the spirit of the Revolution, and the Declaration of Independence. Those documents and events work together to teach us something about the dignity of human beings everywhere: that they are entitled to be free and to rule themselves.

And yet, in and around this, a rich culture of faith and morality teaches us that there is something about life that is more than just getting what we can get for ourselves at all costs. It teaches us that other human beings matter, that we should care for them, that there is

something like transcendent truth out there. This was the view of the founders. There was not perfectly uniform views on religious or moral issues, but there was a general sense that the spirit of liberty, as articulated in the Declaration and made practical in the Constitution, and the spirit of religion could work like a hand in a glove to create a culture of self-rule that was prosperous and humane and had a bright future.

. . . Our most important export has been the Constitution and what it has meant not just for American democracy, but for democracy all across the world.

—

MATTHEW S. HOL-LAND

The legacy of our founding fathers—and it will be the legacy for as long as there is a United States of America—is that human beings possess a profound, inherent, and equal dignity; that they deserve to be governed in a way that is consistent with their dignity; and that they deserve to be governed in a way that gives them a voice in their own fate and their own affairs. The legacy of our founders is the legacy of what we call democracy. It's a legacy of respect for the dignity of the individual.

It is a legacy of respect for the importance of the institutions of civil society, including the family, the church, and the private association. And it's a legacy of belief that the purpose of government is to serve those who are governed—not to serve the interests of the governors. That's the legacy of the American founders. We are not subjects under a king or other potentate. We are citizens. Government exists for us, not the other way around. Our citizens have an obligation to each other and to the country. That's why we are a patriotic people. We recognize that the government we have is a gift—a rare gift—in human history. As such, we owe it our allegiance. We owe it our support. We even need to be willing to give the ultimate sacrifice, should it come to that, as so many of our fellow citizens have done over the centuries. We owe our lives to protect something as precious as a government and a nation based on the proposition that all men are created equal, endowed by their Creator with certain unalienable rights.

—

ROBERT GEORGE

Inset: An illustration of George Washington, Patrick Henry, and Edmund Pendleton on horses on their way to Philadelphia, as delegates to the First Continental Congress.

Dodge, Mary Mapes, St. Nicholas an Illustrated Magazine for Young Folks *(New York: The Century Co., 1886), 509. Florida Center for Instructional Technology, College of Education, University of South Florida.*

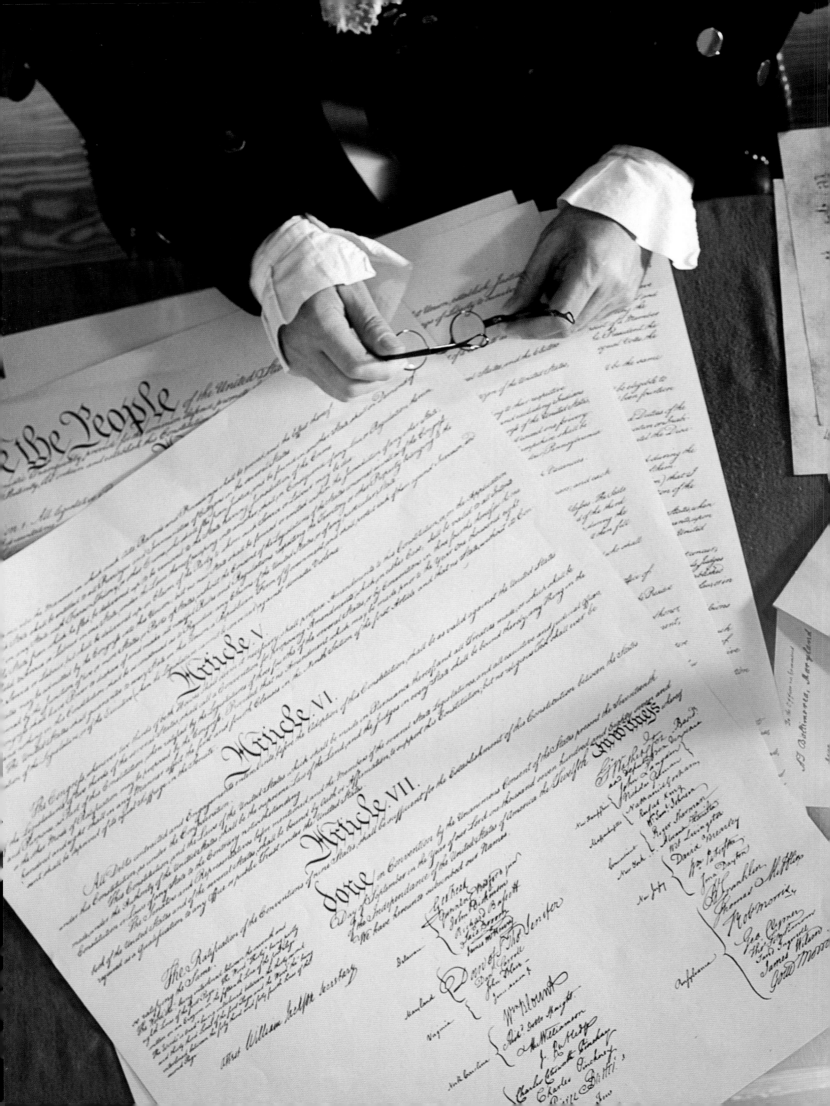

America'ſ FIRST Freedom

Freedom of religion is in many ways the *first* freedom. It was at the cradle of liberty even before there was a United States of America. The great struggle for religious liberty in England, for example, preceded the great struggle for religious liberty in the United States. It's also the first freedom in the sense that it is the first freedom mentioned in the Constitution's Bill of Rights. The very first words of the First Amendment are, "Congress shall make no law respecting an establishment of religion, or prohibiting the free exercise, thereof." These words established our nation as a nation where people could honor their own conscientious convictions and worship God in the way that they believed God wished to be worshipped. And if they did not have a belief in God, they were free to stand aloof from religion.

That has been one of the wonderful legacies of the United States. We honor conscience—especially, and above all, the right to freedom of religion, the right to worship God as one sees fit. And we have learned that our permission for diversity has been a source of unity and strength, not division and weakness. We see people recognizing in each other a certain religious spirit even if they don't share the precise convictions. As a result, we see people of all faiths living together side by side and having respect for each other.

— ———— —

ROBERT GEORGE

All three images from Florida Center for Instructional Technology, College of Education, University of South Florida: The Crew of a Naval Ship in the Revolutionary War Praying before They Head in to Battle. Edward S Ellis, Ellis's History of the United States (Minneapolis: Wester Book Syndicate, 1899), II:697. • The settlement of Rhode Island. Edward S. Ellis, Ellis's History of the United States (Minneapolis: Wester Book Syndicate, 1899), I:189. • A Group of Slaves Attending a Religious Prayer Meeting. J. G. Holland Scribner's Monthly: An Illustrated Magazine for the People (New York: Scriber & Company, 1874), VIII:20.

little doubt that Jefferson and other founders feared the opposite effect, that religious factionalism might imperil the new government.

During his term as president, Jefferson considered the "experiment" in religious freedom that he had helped to create in the new republic and pronounced it good precisely because it had proved conducive to political order and stability. "We have solved by fair example, the great and interesting question whether freedom is compatible with order in government, and obedience to the laws," he wrote to a group of Virginia Baptists later that same year of 1802. "And we have experienced the quiet as well as the comfort which results from leaving everyone to profess freely and openly those principles of religion which are the inductions of his own reason, and the serious convictions of his own inquiries."[79]

The collusion between rationalists and evangelicals—between Thomas Jefferson and Roger Williams—that produced the First Amendment has bequeathed to the United States a vibrant and salubrious religious culture unmatched anywhere in the world. The First Amendment, just as Adam Smith predicted in his 1776 treatise on capitalism, *The Wealth of Nations*, set up a free market for religion, where religious entrepreneurs (to extend the economic metaphor) are free to peddle their wares in the marketplace without either prejudice or favoritism from the state. American history is full of such examples, from Ann Lee, John Humphrey Noyes, and Joseph Smith Jr. to Aimee Semple McPherson, Elijah Muhammad, and Joel Osteen. Put simply and directly, religion has flourished in America precisely because the government (for the most part, at least) has stayed out of the religion business.

Opposite: In June, 1776, a committee was selected to draft a Declaration of Independence. Thomas Jefferson actually wrote the draft, but the other committee members included John Adams, Benjamin Franklin, Roger Sherman and Robert Livingston. It was signed by the Convention delegates on July 4, 1776. *Courtesy of film First Freedom. Photographer, Mark Mabry.*

SELECTED BIBLIOGRAPHY

Beneke, Chris, and Christopher S. Grenda, eds. *The First Prejudice: Religious Tolerance and Intolerance in Early America.* Philadelphia: University of Pennsylvania Press, 2011.

Church, Forrest, ed. *The Separation of Church and State: Writings on a Fundamental Freedom by America's Founders.* Boston: Beacon Press, 2004.

Curry, Thomas J. *The First Freedoms: Church and State in America to the Passage of the First Amendment.* New York: Oxford University Press, 1986.

Drakeman, Donald L. *Church, State, and Original Intent.* Cambridge: Cambridge University Press, 2010.

Fea, John. *Was America Founded as a Christian Nation?: A Historical Introduction.* Louisville, Ky.: Westminster John Knox Press, 2011.

Gaustad, Edwin S. *Church and State in America.* 2nd ed. *Religion in American Life,* Jon Butler and Harry S. Stout, eds. New York: Oxford University Press, 2003.

————. *Faith of the Founders: Religion and the New Nation, 1776–1826.* Foreword by Randall Balmer. Waco, Tex.: Baylor University Press, 2011.

————. *Liberty of Conscience: Roger Williams in America. Library of Religious Biography,* Mark A. Noll and Nathan O. Hatch, eds. Grand Rapids, Mich.: Wm. B. Eerdmans, 1991.

Green, Steven K. *The Bible, the School, and the Constitution: The Clash that Shaped Modern Church–State Doctrine.* New York: Oxford University Press, 2012.

————. *The Second Disestablishment: Church and State in Nineteenth-Century America.* New York: Oxford University Press, 2010.

Hamburger, Philip. *Separation of Church and State.* Cambridge, Mass.: Harvard University Press, 2004.

Holmes, David L. *The Faiths of the Founding Fathers.* New York: Oxford University Press, 2006.

Howe, Mark DeWolfe. *The Garden and the Wilderness: Religion and Government in American Constitutional History.* Chicago: University of Chicago Press, 1967.

Hutson, James H. *Religion and the Founding of the American Republic.* Washington, D.C.: Library of Congress, 1998.

————, ed. *Religion and the New Republic: Faith in the Founding of America.* Lanham, Md.: Rowman & Littlefield, 2000.

————, ed. *The Founders on Religion: A Book of Quotations.* Princeton, N.J.: Princeton University Press, 2005.

Lambert, Frank. *The Founding Fathers and the Place of Religion in America.* Princeton, N.J.: Princeton University Press, 2003.

Larson, Edward J. *A Magnificent Catastrophe: The Tumultuous Election of 1800, America's First Presidential Campaign.* New York: Free Press, 2008.

Meacham, Jon. *American Gospel: God, the Founding Fathers, and the Making of a Nation.* New York: Random House, 2006.

McLoughlin, William G. *Isaac Backus and the American Pietistic Tradition. Library of American Biography,* Oscar Handlin, ed. Boston: Little, Brown & Co., 1967.

Miller, Perry. *Roger Williams: His Contribution to the American Tradition.* Indianapolis: Bobbs-Merrill, 1953.

Morgan, Edmund S. *Roger Williams: The Church and the State.* New York: W. W. Norton, 1967.

Nussbaum, Martha C. *Liberty of Conscience: In Defense of America's Tradition of Religious Equality.* New York: Basic Books, 2008.

Pointer, Richard W. *Protestant Pluralism and the New York Experience: A Study of Eighteenth-Century Diversity.* Bloomington: Indiana University Press, 1988.

Rogasta, John A. *Wellspring of Liberty: How Virginia's Religious Dissenters Helped to Win the American Revolution and Secured Religious Liberty.* New York: Oxford University Press, 2010.

Sanford, Charles B. *The Religious Life of Thomas Jefferson.* Charlottesville: University Press of Virginia, 1984.

Waldman, Steven. *Founding Faith: How Our Founding Fathers Forged a Radical New Approach to Religious Liberty.* New York: Random House, 2008.

Wilson, John F. *Religion and the American Nation: Historiography and History.* Athens: University of Georgia Press, 2003.

Opposite: Fence around Plimoth Plantation, Plymouth, MA. Early colonial villages were usually enclosed with tall fences and had a lookout post for protection against the indigenous people who didn't want them there.

Below: The men of the Puritan village carried their weapons with them so they were always ready for intruders. It would be normal for a colonist to be seen carrying numerous powder horns.

Courtesy of film First Freedom. *Photographer, Mark Mabry.*

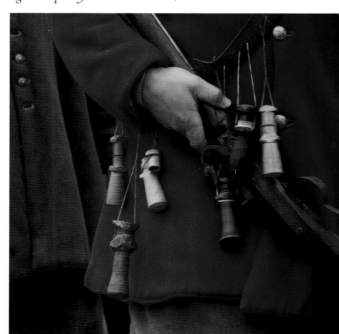

ENDNOTES

1 Benjamin Franklin to George Whitefield, June 6, 1753, in *The Republican*, XII (Nov. 4, 1825), 557.

2 Quoted in John E. Lovell, *The Young Speaker: An Introduction to the United States Speaker* (New Haven, CT, 1849), 165–166. Emphasis in original.

3 Quoted in James P. Moore Jr., *Prayer in America: A Spiritual History of Our Nation* (New York: Doubleday, 2005), 70.

4 Edward Johnson, "Wonder-Working Providence of Sion's Savior in New England," in *The Puritans in America: A Narrative Anthology*, Alan Heimert and Andrew Delbanco, eds. (Cambridge, MA: Harvard University Press, 1985), 116.

5 Franklin Jameson, ed., *Narratives of New Netherland, 1609–1664* (New York, 1909), 392.

6 Jameson, ed., *Narratives of New Netherland*, 123–125.

7 John Winthrop, "A Model of Christian Charity" (1630), in *Puritans in America*, Heimert and Delbanco, eds., 91.

8 John Cotton, "A Discourse About Civil Government," in *Church and State in American History: Key Documents, Decisions, and Commentary from the Past Three Centuries*, 3rd ed., John F. Wilson and Donald L. Drakeman, eds. (Boulder, CO: Westview Press, 2003), 19–20.

9 Roger Williams, "Queries of Highest Consideration" (1644), in *Church and State in American History*, Wilson and Drakeman, eds., 22.

10 Quoted in Daniel L. Dreisbach, "Thomas Jefferson, a Mammoth Cheese, and the 'Wall of Separation,'" in *Religion and the New Republic: Faith in the Founding of America*, James H. Hutson, ed. (Lanham, MD: Rowman & Littlefield, 2000), 85. Scholars disagree about whether Jefferson was directly aware of Williams's "wall of separation" metaphor.

11 Quoted in Edwin S. Gaustad, *Liberty of Conscience: Roger Williams in America* (Grand Rapids, MI: Wm. B. Eerdmans, 1991), 38.

12 "The Charter of Rhode Island and Providence Plantations" (1663), in *Church and State in American History*, Wilson and Drakeman, eds., 30–31.

13 John Winthrop, *A Short Story of the Rise, Reign, and Ruine of the Antinomians, Familists & Libertines*, in *The Antinomian Controversy, 1636–1638: A Documentary History*, David D. Hall, ed. (Middletown, CT: Wesleyan University Press, 1968), 273.

14 Quoted in Edwin S. Gaustad, *Church and State in America*, 2nd ed. (New York: Oxford University Press, 2003), 21.

15 "Flushing Remonstrance," 1657, in *Church and State in the Modern Age: A Documentary History*, ed. J. F. Maclear (New York: Oxford University Press, 1995), 49.

16 "Company Directors' Instructions to Stuyvesant," 1663, in *Church and State in the Modern Age*, Maclear, ed., 49.

17 Quoted in George Petrie, *Church and State in Early Maryland*, vol. 4 of *Johns Hopkins University Studies in Historical and Political Science*, Herbert B. Adams, ed. (Baltimore, 1892), 220.

18 Letter, Lord Cornbury to the Society for the Propagation of the Gospel, November 29, 1707, S.P.G. Records, Letterbook Series A, no. CLV; letter, Lord Cornbury to the Society for the Propagation of the Gospel, September 22, 1705, S.P.G. Records, Letterbook Series A, Vol. 2, no. CXXXI.

19 "Mary Dyer, Letter to the Massachusetts General Court After She Had Received the Sentence of Death, 1659," in *The Female Experience: An American Documentary*, Gerda Lerner, ed. (New York: Oxford University Press, 1977), 473.

20 Jonathan Parsons, "Account of the Revival at Lyme," in *The Great Awakening: Documents Illustrating the Crisis and Its Consequences*, Alan Heimert and Perry Miller, eds. (Indianapolis: Bobbs-Merrill, 1967), 190. Emphasis in original.

21 Samuel Willard, "The Peril of the Times Displayed," 1700, in *The Great Awakening: Documents on the Revival of Religion, 1740–1745*, Richard L. Bushman, ed. (New York: Atheneum, 1970), 6.

22 *Ecclesiastical Records: State of New York*, 7 vols., Edward T. Corwin, ed. (Albany, 1901–1916), III, 2182–2183. On Frelinghuysen's career in New Jersey, see Randall Balmer, *A Perfect Babel of Confusion: Dutch Religion and English Culture in the Middle Colonies* (New York: Oxford University Press, 1989), chap. 5.

23 Quoted in James Tanis, *Dutch Calvinistic Pietism in the Middle Colonies: A Study in the Life and Theology of Theodorus Jacobus Frelinghuysen* (The Hague: Martinus Nijhoff, 1967), 54.

24 The Spiritual Travels of Nathan Cole," 1741, in *The Great Awakening*, Bushman, ed., 67–68.

25 Franklin's autobiography is widely available, both in printed and electronic form; one source is Benjamin Franklin, *Benjamin Franklin: His Life*, D. H. Montgomery, ed. (Boston, 1888), 137–138.

26 Jonathan Parsons, "Account of the Revival at Lyme," in *The Great Awakening*, Heimert and Miller, eds., 198.

27 Isaac Backus, *An Appeal to the Public for Religious Liberty*, in *The Separation of Church and State: Writings on a Fundamental Freedom by America's Founders*, Forrest Church, ed. (Boston: Beacon Press, 2004), 21.

28 "Davenport Rebuked in Boston: The Declaration of A Number of the Associated Pastors of Boston and Charles-Town," 1742, in *The Great Awakening*, Bushman, ed., 51.

29 Solomon Stoddard, "Defects of Preachers Reproved," 1723, in *The Great Awakening*, Bushman, ed., 15.

30 Quoted in Harry S. Stout, *The New England Soul: Preaching and Religious Culture in Colonial New England* (New York: Oxford University Press, 1986), 298.

31 Quoted in William Wirt Henry, *Patrick Henry: Life, Correspondence and Speeches* (New York, 1891), 119.

32 "Colonial Criticism of the Appeal," 1768, in *Church and State in American History: Key Documents, Decisions, and Commentary from the Past Three Centuries*, 3rd ed., John F. Wilson and Donald L. Drakeman, eds. (Boulder, CO: Westview Press, 2003), 59.

33 John M. Mulder, "William Livingston: Propagandist against Episcopacy," *Journal of Presbyterian History*, 54 (1976):83–104.

34 "Grievances Against the Connecticut Establishment," 1751, in *Church and State in American History*, Wilson and Drakeman, eds., 41–42.

35 Quoted in Steven Waldman, *Founding Faith: How Our Founding Fathers Forged a Radical New Approach to Religious Liberty* (New York: Random House, 2008), 100.

36 Quoted in Edwin S. Gaustad, *The Great Awakening in New England* (New York: Harper & Row, 1957), 110.

37 Quoted in John Fea, *Was America Founded as a Christian Nation?: A Historical Introduction* (Louisville, KY: Westminster John Knox Press, 2011), 240. Emphasis in original.

38 Quoted in Arthur Lyon Cross, *The Anglican Episcopate and the American Colonies* (New York, 1902), 142, 145.

39 Quoted in Cross, *Anglican Episcopate and the American Colonies*, 159.

40 Benjamin Franklin, "A Comparison of the Conduct of Ancient Jews and Anti-federalists in the United States of America," in *The Founders on Religion: A Book of Quotations*, James H. Hutson, ed. (Princeton, NJ: Princeton University Press, 2005), 76–77.

41 Quoted in *The Friend: A Religious and Literary Journal*, Dec. 1, 1900, 154.

42 Ibid.; Psalm 35:1 (KJV).

43 "Address of the General Congress to the Inhabitants of the Province of Québec," in William Kingsford, *The History of Canada* (Toronto, 1892), 264.

44 Quoted in Jared Sparks, *The Writings of George Washington; Being his Correspondence, Addresses, Messages, and Other Papers, Official and Private*, vol. 12 (Boston, 1837), 154.

45 Quoted in Chris Beneke, "The 'Catholic Spirit Prevailing in Our Country': America's Moderate Religious Revolution," in *The First Prejudice: Religious Tolerance and Intolerance in Early America*, Chris Beneke and Christopher S. Grenda, eds. (Philadelphia: University of Pennsylvania Press, 2011), 276.

46 Quoted in *The Founders on Religion*, Hutson, ed., 211, 206.

47 Quoted in Gary Scott Smith, *Faith and the Presidency: From George Washington to George W. Bush* (New York: Oxford University Press, 2006), 29; "George Washington to the President of Congress, December 31, 1775," in *The Founders on Religion*, Hutson, ed., 47.

48 *Maxims of George Washington* (New York, 1894), 350.

49 Quoted in J. Adams, *Sermon, Preached in St. Michael's Church, Charleston, February 13ᵗʰ, 1833, Before the Convention of the Protestant Episcopal Church of the Diocese of South-Carolina*, 2ⁿᵈ ed. (Charleston, SC, 1833), 42.

50 Quoted in Vincent Phillip Muñoz, "James Madison's Principle of Religious Liberty," *American Political Science Review*, 91 (Feb. 2003), 17–32.

51 F. Greene, *The Writings of the Late Elder John Leland, Including Some Events in His Life* (New York, 1845), 118.

52 John Adams to Francis van der Kemp, Oct. 2, 1818, in *The Founders on Religion*, Hutson, ed., 134.

53 George Washington, "To the Legislature of the State of Connecticut, October, 1789," in Jared Sparks, *The Writings of George Washington; Being his Correspondence, Addresses, Messages, and Other Papers, Official and Private*, vol. 12 (Boston, 1837), 169–170.

54 "Jefferson's Act for Establishing Religious Freedom," 1786, in *Church and State in American History: Key Documents, Decisions, and Commentary from the Past Three Centuries*, 3ʳᵈ ed., John F. Wilson and Donald L. Drakeman, eds. (Boulder, CO: Westview Press, 2003), 68.

55 "General Assessment Bill," in Charles Fenton James, *Documentary History of the Struggle for Religious Liberty in Virginia* (Lynchburg, VA, 1900), 129.

56 Letter, James Madison to James Monroe, April 12, 1785, in James, *Documentary History of the Struggle for Religious Liberty in Virginia*, 130; "Baptists Stand Firm," in Ibid., 131; Baptist General Committee, in Ibid., 138.

57 "Assessment Bill Losing Ground," in James, *Documentary History of the Struggle for Religious Liberty in Virginia*, 135.

58 "Madison's *Memorial and Remonstrance*," in *Church and State in American History*, Wilson and Drakeman, 63–67.

59 "Jefferson's Act for Establishing Religious Freedom" (1786), in *Church and State in American History*, Wilson and Drakeman, eds., 69.

60 *The Records of the Federal Convention of 1787*, Max Farrand, ed., vol. 2 (New Haven, CT, 1911), 642.

61 Quoted in John R. Vile, *The Constitutional Convention of 1787: A Comprehensive Encyclopedia of America's Founding*, vol. 2 (Santa Barbara, CA: ABC-CLIO, 2005), 272.

62 Letter, George Washington to Edward Newenham, October 20, 1792, in Jared Sparks, *The Writings of George Washington; Being his Correspondence, Addresses, Messages, and Other Papers, Official and Private*, vol. 12 (Boston, 1837), 404–405.

63 Quoted in Thomas G. West, *Vindicating the Founders: Race, Sex, Class, and Justice in the Origins of America* (Lanham, MD: Rowman & Littlefield, 1997), 149.

64 Quoted in Martha C. Nussbaum, *Liberty of Conscience: In Defense of America's Tradition of Religious Equality* (New York: Basic Books, 2008), 89.

65 Benjamin Rush to John Adams, June 15, 1789, in *The Founders on Religion: A Book of Quotations*, James H. Hutson, ed. (Princeton, NJ: Princeton University Press, 2005), 77.

66 James Madison, "A Detached Memorandum," in *The Separation of Church and State: Writings on a Fundamental Freedom by America's Founders*, Forrest Church, ed. (Boston: Beacon Press, 2004), 139.

67 John Adams to Benjamin Rush, June 12, 1812, in *The Founders on Religion*, Hutson, ed., 100–101.

68 Quoted in Edward J. Larson, *A Magnificent Catastrophe: The Tumultuous Election of 1800, America's First Presidential Campaign* (New York: Free Press, 2007), 173.

69 Quoted in "Private Character of Thomas Jefferson," *Living Age*, August 31, 1861, 520.

70 Thomas Jefferson to Benjamin Rush, April 21, 1803, in *The Portable Thomas Jefferson*, Merrill D. Peterson, ed. (New York: Penguin Books, 1975), n.p.

71 Quoted in Paul K. Conklin, "The Religious Pilgrimage of Thomas Jefferson," in *Jeffersonian Legacies*, Peter S. Onuf, ed. (Charlottesville: University Press of Virginia, 1993), 44. Emphasis in original.

72 Quoted in Joseph P. Hester, *The Ten Commandments: A Handbook of Religious, Legal, and Social Issues* (Jefferson, NC: MacFarland & Co., 2003), 136; Benjamin Rush to Granville Sharp, April 27, 1784, in *The Founders on Religion*, Hutson, ed., 98.

73 Thomas Jefferson to Jacob Delamotta, September 1, 1820, in *The Founders on Religion*, Hutson, ed., 136–137.

74 *Selected Writings of James Madison*, Ralph Ketchum, ed. (Indianapolis: Hackett, 2006), 307.

75 Thomas Jefferson, "A Wall of Separation," in *The Separation of Church and State: Writings on a Fundamental Freedom by America's Founders*, Forrest Church, ed. (Boston: Beacon Press, 2004), 127.

76 Most of this narrative is derived from C. A. Browne, "Elder John Leland and the Mammoth Cheshire Cheese," *Agricultural History*, 18 (Oct. 1944), 145–153. My assertion that Jefferson received the cheese earlier in the day is implicit from one of the contemporaneous accounts quoted in Ibid., 151. The account reads, in part, "The great cheese arrived last night and this morning was presented to President Jefferson as a New Year's gift."

77 Quoted in Browne, "Elder John Leland and the Mammoth Cheshire Cheese," 149, 150.

78 Thomas Jefferson, "A Wall of Separation," in *Separation of Church and State*, Church, ed., 130.

79 Thomas Jefferson to the Baptist Association at Chesterfield, Virginia, November 21, 1808, in *The Writings of Thomas Jefferson*, vol. 16 (Washington, DC, 1904–1905), 320. I have addressed this collusion between Roger Williams and Thomas Jefferson in *Blessed Assurance: A History of Evangelicalism in America* (Boston: Beacon Press, 1999), chap. 2.

John and Abigail Adams were devoted to each other; historians gained a wealth of historical notes from their letters to each other.

Courtesy of film First Freedom. *Photographer, Mark Mabry.*

QUOTED SCHOLARS

Numerous scholars were interviewed for the film documentary. Some of their dialogue has been included in the book as sidebars and captions. This list includes a brief accreditation for each of those scholars:

JON MEACHAM, Historian, Pulitzer author of *American Gospel*

PATRICIA BONOMI, professor emeritus, New York University; historian, author of *Under The Cope of Heaven*

JOHN HOPE FRANKLIN (deceased), professor, Duke University; historian, author of *From Slavery to Freedom*, namesake of John Hope Franklin Center for Interdisciplinary and International Studies, Duke University

CHARLES ALLEN, Puritan expert, historian, author of *Out of Captivity*

DAVID L. HOLMES, professor, College of William and Mary; historian, author of *Faiths of the Founding Fathers*

George Washington's property at Mt. Vernon.

Courtesy of film First Freedom. *Photographer, Mark Mabry.*

JAMES HUTSON, archivist, Library of Congress; historian, author of *The Founders on Religion*

GORDON S. WOOD, professor, Brown University; historian, Pulitzer author of *The Creation of the American Revolution*

MATTHEW S. HOLLAND, president, Utah Valley University; historian, author of *Bonds of Affection: Civic Charity and the Making of America*

NATHAN O. HATCH, president, Wake Forest University; historian, Pulitzer author of *The Democratization of Christianity*

JON BUTLER, dean, Graduate School of Arts and Sciences, Yale University; historian, author of *Awash in a Sea of Faith*

DOUG BRINKLEY, professor, Rice University; historian, scriptwriter, author of *The Reagan Diaries* and numerous other historical books

JULIE FENSTER, historian, scriptwriter, author of *Parish Priest* and numerous other American heritage books and articles

JACK WELCH, professor, J. Reuben Clark School of Law, Brigham Young University; historian, author of *Lectures on Religion and the Founding of the American Republic*

RICHARD BUSHMAN, professor emeritus, Columbia University; historian, author of *The Great Awakening: Documents on the Revival of Religion 1740-1745*

FORREST CHURCH (deceased), pastor, All Souls Church, Manhattan, NY; historian, author of *So Help Me God: The Founding Fathers and the First Great Battle Over Church and State*

COKIE ROBERTS, senior analyst, NPR Radio; Emmy award-winning journalist, historian, author of *The Women Who Shaped Our Nation*

ROBERT GEORGE, professor, director, James Madison Institute, Princeton University; historian, author of *Natural Law and Public Reason*

DANIEL MARIASCHIN, executive vice president, B'Nai B'rith International

CHARLES HAYNES, director, Religious Education Project, Newseum; senior scholar, First Amendment Center

CRAIG K. MANSCILL, professor, Brigham Young University; historian, author

ROBERT MILLET, professor, Brigham Young University; historian, author